JEWS WHO ROCK

ieBoys Beck RayBenson ERICBLOOM MikeBloomfield MarcBola
OND AdamDurwitz Bob Dylan JakobDylan dannyelfman DONAL
yFriedman JUSTINEFRISCHMANN KennyG ArtGarfunkel
RICHARDHELL GregHetson Peter Himmelman SusannaHoffs Sco
leKing MarkKnopfler ALKooper LennyKRAVITZ GettyLe
e GARY LUCAS Mamas and the Papas Barry Manilov
laren MCSEARCH NateMendel BetteMidler KeithMORRI
l Phranc JoeyRamone LouReed JonathanRichman DavidLe
ulSimon Slash HillelSlovakDeeSNIDERJillSobule PhilSpe

rb Alpert Judah Bauer Beastie Boys Beck Ray Benson ERIC BLOOM
mmy Davis Jr. NEIL DIAMOND Adam Durwitz Bob Dylan Ja
son Finn Alan Freed Marty Friedman JUSTINE FRISCHMANN Ke
eter Green Brett Gurewitz RICHARD HELL Greg Hetson Peter Hi
eve Katz Len NY Kaye Carole King Mark Knopfler AL Koop
Loeb Courtney Love GARY LUCAS Mamas and the Papa
nfred Mann Malcolm McClaren MC SEARCH Nate Mendel Be
phen Perkins Monique Powell Phranc Joey Ramone Lou Reed
ne Simmons CARLY SIMON Paul Simon Slash Hillel Slovak Dee S

JEWS WHO ROCK

GUY OSEARY

Foreword by Ben Stiller

Afterword by Perry Farrell

Mike Shea, Editor, Photo Digger, and Scavenger Hunter

St. Martin's Griffin ❦ *New York*

www.stmartins.com

Production Editor: Shana Carter

Book design by Tim Hall

ISBN 0-312-27267-7

First Edition: January 2001

10 9 8 7 6 5 4 3 2 1

Jews Who Rock is dedicated to my mother, Gila, and to my father, Yossi. It is also dedicated to my best friend, partner in life, and the most rocking Jew of all, Madonna.

rbAlpert JudahBauer BeastieBoys Beck RayBenson ERICBLOO
mmyDavis Jr. NEIL DIAMOND AdamDurwitz Bob Dylan Ja
asonFinn AlanFreed MartyFriedman JUSTINEFRISCHMANN Ke
eterGreen BrettGurewitz RICHARDHELL GregHetson Peter Hi
eveKatz LenNYKaye CaroleKing MarkKnopfler ALKoo
aLoeb CourtneyLove GARY LUCAS Mamas and the Pap
nfredMann Malcolm McClaren MC SEARCH NateMendel Be
ephenPerkins MoniquePowell Phranc JoeyRamone LouReed
ne Simmons CARLYSIMON PaulSimon Slash Hillel Slovak Dee

Contents

Acknowledgments

Thank you to everyone who helped me work on this book: Ben Stiller, Adam Sandler, Jakob Dylan, Perry Farrell, Anthony Kiedis, Lenny Kravitz, Mike Diamond, David Geffen, Dan Green, Ken Hertz, Harvey Hertz, Sophia Tsilidas, Scott Cooke, Bill Vuylsteke, Shelly Venemann, Elizabeth Beier, Michael Connor, and all of St. Martin's Press. David Vigliano, Mike Shea, and the *Alternative Press* crew, and Scott Sandler, Jonathan Looghran, Ari Emanuel, Nick Stevens, and Josh Richman all provided invaluable assistance. A big thanks to Chris Rock for letting me use his last name in the title of this book.

Additional material and editing by Jason Pettigrew and Rob Cherry at *Alternative Press* magazine.

Additional research and material by Edwin Camacho.

Mike Shea would also like to thank Peter Grossman/Retna, Helen Ashford/Michael Ochs Archives, Jenny Barbee/Shooting Star, Karen Moss/Warner Brothers Records, Sheila Richman/Island Def Jam Records, and Edwin Camacho for the home-stretch run. And, especially, Guy Oseary, for the chance to work on such a great project.

rb Alpert Judah Bauer Beastie Boys Beck Ray Benson ERIC BLOO
mmy Davis Jr. NEIL DIAMOND Adam Durwitz Bob Dylan Ja
asonFinn AlanFreed MartyFriedman JUSTINE FRISCHMANN Ker
eterGreen BrettGurewitz RICHARDHELL GregHetson Peter Hir
veKatz LenNYKaye CaroleKing MarkKnopfler ALKoo
Loeb CourtneyLove GARY LUCAS Mamas and the Papa
nfredMann Malcolm McClaren MC SEARCH NateMendel Be
phenPerkins MoniquePowell Phranc JoeyRamone LouReed
e Simmons CARLYSIMON PaulSimon Slash Hillel Slovak Dees

Foreword

by Ben Stiller

In 1978, I was bar mitzvahed at the Stephen Wise Free Synagogue on West Sixty-eighth Street in Manhattan. It was a midsized event as those things go, no party at the nearby Tavern on the Green, which at the time was *the* place to celebrate after becoming a man. We had our party in the underground auditorium of the synagogue. It was much less ostentatious and much more "homey," my mom said.

I invited most of my eighth-grade friends, and my parents invited most of their relatives. The only party crasher I recall was Warner Wolf, the local sportscaster, who was a frequent Saturday morning shul attendee. My haftorah never made his highlight reel, probably because, as I later learned from the cantor who tutored me for six months prior, I "modulated" three octaves during the singing part. It wasn't until years later that I understood the meaning of "modulation." All I knew at the time was that I sang out of key.

I was not born a singer.

But I, like many kids my age, was a big rock and roll fan. At thirteen, I was in a band called Capital Punishment, anchoring the rhythm section of our guitar-based quartet, playing the white Slingerland drum kit my mother had shelled out for the previous Christmas (don't ask—my parents sent mixed messages).

The Beatles, the Who, and Bruce Springsteen were my musical heroes of choice, with an occasional foray into Joe Jackson territory. For me, my bar mitzvah was not about coming of age; it was about Capital Punishment's first gig.

We covered "Hey Jude" at the after party. Needless to say, my great-uncle Isidore was not rocking out. My father panicked, misunderstanding the lyrics and thinking that our lead singer was belting out "Hey Jew" to a roomful of Holocaust survivors and their progeny. I will never forget the perplexed expressions of those poor folks, who came all the way in from the far reaches of Brooklyn and North Miami to dance the hora and ended up having to sit through our under-rehearsed "My Generation," featuring our bassist, Jonathan, gamely attempting to outdo John Entwistle's masterful solos and failing miserably.

That is as close to being a Jew who rocks as I ever became; Capital Punishment disbanded when Jonathan transferred to a school across town for being caught with a bag of pot (which he had stolen from his dad) in his bass case, and when I realized that drummers should actually have a sense of rhythm.

I also think that one of the reasons we broke up was that I had always harbored an almost unconscious belief that because I was Jewish and from New York, and did not have an Iggy Pop rock-star physique, I was not really allowed to be a rock star. "Rock and roll" and "Jew" just never seemed to go together. Usually it was "Jew" and "intellectual," or "rock star" and "heroin addict." It wasn't till years later that I realized you could combine all those wonderful qualities into one incredibly self-destructive genius. There are quite a few of those inside, so read on!

At the very least, this book is here to show you that.

We as creative entities in the twenty-first century, must come to see that we need not be categorized by outdated ethnic stereotypes. Punk rockers can eat gefilte fish if they want to, African-American hip-hop artists can enjoy Woody Allen as much as Jews can rock, if that's what they choose.

One word of advice, however. Select your venue carefully. I wouldn't recommend the auditorium of the Stephen Weiss Synagogue for the next Beastie Boys show. The acoustics suck.

Introduction

The original inspiration for this book came when my friend Josh Richman gave me a book called *Jews in Sports* as a Hanukah gift. I instantly thought about all of the Jewish artists who were in rock, and knew how outstanding a book about them could be.

I was born in Israel and moved to the United States when I was eight years old. I can still remember how excited I was when I learned that some of my favorite musicians were Jewish—it made me feel proud of my Judaic background and where I came from.

There are a lot of kids out there who might feel alone because they're the only Jewish person in their school or community. Discovering that a favorite musician is Jewish might give them a reason to feel positive about their culture, religion, and themselves.

I wrote this book to honor and celebrate these rockin' Jews . . . I give you *Jews Who Rock.*

loomfield MarcBolan MICHAELBoltonIgorCavaleraLEONARD CO
an dennyeldman DONALDFAGEN PerryFarrellNickFeldman DougFeig
rtGarfunkel AdamGaynor GerryGoffin NINAGORDO
n SusannaHoffs ScottIan BillyJOEL MickJONES Ira Kapla
nnyKRAVITZ GettyLee JerryLeiber & Mike Stoller KEITHLev
rry Manilow DickManitoba BarryMANN Cynthia W
dler KeithMORRIS Randy Newman NOFX LauraNYRO **xiii** ILO
thanRichman DavidLeeRoth ADAMSANDLER NeilSEDAKAJosh Sil
JillSobule PhilSpector PaulStanley ChrisSTEINSteveSTE

The Chanukah Song

by Adam Sandler

Put on your yarmulke
Here comes Chanukah
So much funukah
To celebrate Chanukah
Chanukah is the festival of lights
Instead of the day of presents, we have eight crazy nights

When you feel like the only kid in town without a Christmas tree
Here's a list of people who are Jewish just like you and me
David Lee Roth lights the menorah
So do Kirk Douglas, James Caan, and the late Dinah Shore-ah

Guess who eats together at the Carnegie Deli
Bowser from Sha Na Na and Arthur Fonzerelli
Paul Newman's half Jewish, Goldie Hawn's half too
Put them together, what a fine looking Jew

You don't need "Deck the Halls" or "Jingle Bell Rock"
'Cause you can spin a dreidel with Captain Kirk or Mr. Spock—both
Jewish

Put on your yarmulke
It's time for Chanukah
The owner of the Seattle Supersonics celebrates Chanukah

bAlpert Judah Bauer Beastie Boys Beck Ray Benson ERIC BLOOM
umy Davis Jr. NEIL DIAMOND Adam Durwitz Bob Dylan Jak
sohn Finn Alan Freed Marty Friedman JUSTINE FRISCHMANN Ken
ter Green Brett Gurewitz RICHARD HELL Greg Hetson Peter Him
ve Katz Lenny Kaye Carole King Mark Knopfler AL Koop
Loeb Courtney Love GARY LUCAS Mamas and the Papa
nfred Mann Malcolm McClaren MC SEARCH Nate Mendel Be
phen Perkins Monique Powell Phranc Joey Ramone Lou Ree
e Simmons CARLY SIMON Paul Simon Slash Hillel Slovak Dees

O.J. Simpson, not a Jew
But guess who is? Hall of Famer Rod Carew — he converted

We got Ann Landers and her sister Dear Abby
Harrison Ford's a quarter Jewish — not too shabby

Some people think that Ebenezer Scrooge is
Well he's not, but guess who is
All three Stooges
So many Jews in showbiz
Tom Cruise isn't, but I heard his agent is

Tell your friend Veronica
It's time to celebrate Chanukah
I hope I get a harmonicah
On this lovely, lovely Chanukah
So drink your gin and tonicah
And smoke your marijuanicah
If you really, really wannakah
Have a happy, happy, happy, happy Chanukah
Happy Chanukah

loomfield MarcBolan MICHAELBoltonIgorCavaleraLEONARD C
an dannyelfman DONALDFAGEN PerryFarrellNickFeldman DougFei
ArtGarfunkel AdamGaynor GerryGoffin NINAGORD
n SusannaHoffs ScottIan BillyJOEL MickJONES Ira Kapl
nnyKRAVITZ GettyLee JerryLeiber & Mike Stoller KEITHLe
rry Manilow DickManitoba BarryMANN Cynthia W
idler KeithMORRIS Randy Newman NOFX LauraNYRO ILO
thanRichman DavidLeeRoth ADAMSANDLER NeilSEDAKAJosh Sil
JillSobule PhilSpector PaulStanley ChrisSTEINSTEVESTE

bAlpert JudahBauer BeastieBoys Beck RayBenson ERICBLOOM
nmyDavisJr. NEIL DIAMOND AdamDurwitz Bob Dylan Jak
sonFinn AlanFreed MartyFriedman JUSTINEFRISCHMANN Ken
terGreen BrettGurewitz RICHARDHELL GregHetson Peter Him
veKatz LenNYKaye CaroleKing MarkKnopfler ALKoop
Loeb CourtneyLove GARY LUCAS Mamas and the Papa
nfredMann Malcolm McClaren MC SEARCH NateMendel Bet
ohenPerkins MoniquePowell Phranc JoeyRamone LouReed
e Simmons CARLYSIMON PaulSimon Slash Hillel Slovak DeeS

JEWS WHO ROCK

rb Alpert Judah Bauer Beastie Boys Beck Ray Benson ERIC BLOO
mmy Davis Jr. NEIL DIAMOND Adam Durwitz Bob Dylan Ja
isonFinn Alan Freed Marty Friedman JUSTINE FRISCHMANN Ker
eterGreen Brett Gurewitz RICHARD HELL Greg Hetson Peter Hi
ve Katz LennY Kaye Carole King Mark Knopfler AL Koo
a Loeb Courtney Love GARY LUCAS Mamas and the Papa
nfred Mann Malcolm McClaren MC SEARCH Nate Mendel Be
phen Perkins Monique Powell Phranc Joey Ramone Lou Reed
ie Simmons CARLY SIMON Paul Simon Slash Hillel Slovak Dee S

Herb Alpert

Born: March 31, 1935 — Los Angeles, CA

Talent: Trumpeter/songwriter/producer/record label founder

The Road to Fame: While under contract as a recording artist for RCA in 1962, Herb formed A&M Records with his friend Jerry Moss. Switching to his own label, his Latin-tinged backing band, the Tijuana Brass, hit the big time in 1965 with "A Taste of Honey" from *Whipped Cream and Other Delights*. Four more number-one albums followed until Herb hit a slump in 1969. Nonetheless, the label's prosperity allowed Herb to continue recording at his leisure. Though Herb scored sporadic comeback hits throughout the 1970s and 1980s, the crowning achievement of his career came in 1990 when he and Moss sold A&M to PolyGram for over half a billion dollars. In addition to founding a new label with Moss (Almo Sounds), Herb went on to produce Broadway plays, record new albums, and exhibit his paintings.

The Music: Hit Albums: *Whipped Cream and Other Delights* (1965), *Going Places* (1965), *What Now My Love* (1966), *S.R.O.* (1966), *Sounds Like* (1967), *Herb Alpert's Ninth* (1967), *Rise* (1979), *Keep Your Eye on Me* (1987)

Did You Know? Herb cowrote the Sam Cooke hits "Wonderful World" and "Sixteen" with producer Lou Adler.

Early A&M successes included the Carpenters, Cat Stevens, Joe Cocker, and Sergio Mendes & Brasil '66.

Herb's 1987 hit single "Diamonds" featured vocals by A&M superstar Janet Jackson.

Herb produced the Broadway hits *Angels in America* and *Jelly's Last Jam*.

Herb became a philanthropist with the founding of the Herb Alpert Foundation in the mid-1990s.

Simins, Bauer, Spencer

Judah Bauer and Russell Simins

The Jon Spencer
Blues Explosion

Born: Judah: 1973—Appleton, WI
Russell: 1961—Long Island, NY

Talent: Judah: Guitarist
Russell: Drummer

The Road to Fame: Upon their departure from the New York–based trash-rock band the Honeymoon Killers in 1991, Judah and Russell joined singer/guitarist Jon Spencer (formerly of New York City attitude kings, Pussy Galore) to form the Jon Spencer Blues Explosion, a post-punk, blues-inspired juggernaut. After recording their self-titled debut for Caroline in 1992, the group signed with Matador the following year and eventually landed a coveted spot on a Beastie Boys tour. The resulting exposure, combined with MTV airplay, led to success beyond the underground realm.

The Music: Albums: *The Jon Spencer Blues Explosion* (1992), *Extra Width* (1993), *Orange* (1994), *Experimental Remixes* (1995), *A Ass Pocket of Whiskey* (1996), *Now I Got Worry* (1996), *Acme* (1998), *Xtra Acme USA* (1999)

Did you know? The group recorded *A Ass Pocket of Whiskey* with authentic Delta bluesman R. L. Burnside.

Before picking up the guitar in his late teens, Judah was a bebop saxophonist.

Russell's first drum kit—the same one he currently uses—was formerly owned by drumming legend Buddy Rich.

Judah has a side project with his brother Donovan called Twenty Miles. They have released records on the indie labels In The Red and Fat Possum.

Russell had a side project, Butter 08, which featured the participation of members from such hip New York City bands as Cibo Matto and Skeleton Key.

In the video for "Talk About the Blues," look-alike actors stand in for the band's members. John C. Reilly (*Boogie Nights*) doubled for Russell, and Giovanni Ribisi (*The Mod Squad*) stood in for Judah.

Yauch, Horowitz, and Diamond

Beastie Boys

Born: Mike D: Born Michael Diamond, November 20, 1965—Upper West Side, NYC

MCA: Born Adam Yauch, August 5, 1967—Brooklyn Heights, NYC

Ad-Rock: Born Adam Horovitz, October 31, 1966—Upper West Side, NYC

Talent: Rappers/songwriters/ musicians

The Road to Fame: Middle class Jews Diamond and Yauch formed the original Beastie Boys as a hardcore punk band in 1981. Their drummer and guitarist left in 1983, just as Horovitz had folded his punk band, the Young and the Useless, to join the group and help them make their transition to rap. In 1984, the Beasties signed with Columbia's Def Jam Records and released *Licensed to Ill*, the best-selling rap album of the 1980s, two years later. After a dispute with their label in 1988, they signed with Capitol and were teamed with the Dust Brothers, acclaimed producers of cutting-edge music. Their groundbreaking follow-up, *Paul's Boutique*, failed commercially but earned them cult status. The underground fame soon paid off and the Beasties reemerged in the '90s with their own label, Grand Royal, and a series of best-selling albums.

The Music: **Breakthrough Hit**: "Fight for Your Right (To Party)" (1986)

Best-Selling LP: *Licensed to Ill* (1986)

Other Hit Singles: "Sabotage" (1994), "Sure Shot" (1994), "Intergalactic" (1997)

Did you know? The Beastie Boys opened for Madonna during her *Like a Virgin* Tour and were nearly booed off the stage for their comically profane stage antics.

Licensed to Ill was the fastest selling debut in Columbia Records history (750,000 copies in its first six weeks). It remains the Beasties's best-selling disc, with sales of over 8 million.

The Beasties were arrested, sued, and accused of inciting riots during their 1987 tour.

"Cookie Puss," their first underground hit single, was based on a prank phone call the group made to a Carvel ice cream store.

Ad-Rock's father is New York playwright Israel Horovitz.

The band founded the Tibetan Freedom Concerts, a series of benefit shows that call attention to the persecution of the people of Tibet.

Beck

Born: Beck David Campbell, July 8, 1970—Los Angeles, CA

Talent: Singer/songwriter/instrumentalist/producer

The Road to Fame: With the indie hit "Loser," Beck rose out of relative obscurity in 1994 to become one of the decade's most celebrated rock-and-roll icons. After a brief bidding war, Beck signed with DGC and released *Mellow Gold*, an album showcasing his eclectic amalgamation of gospel, rap, pop, punk, and classic rock. Following his participation in Lollapalooza in 1995, he released *Odelay*, considered by critics and listeners alike to be 1996's Album of the Year. In 1998, he recorded *Mutations*, a sample- and drum-loop-free album with an acoustic feel.

The Music: Albums: *Mellow Gold* (1994), *Stereopathetic Soul Manure* (1994), *One Foot in the Grave* (1994), *Odelay* (1996), *Mutations* (1998), *Midnite Vultures* (1999)

Did you know? Beck took his mother's maiden name, Hansen, as his new last name after his parents divorced.

Beck became involved with the anti-folk movement—led by Paleface, Michelle Shocked, and Cindy Lee Berryhill—during a bus ride to New York.

DGC allows Beck to release experimental records on indie labels, such as *Stereopathetic Soul Manure* (Flipside Records) and *One Foot in the Grave* (K Records).

Beck used only a portable eight-track recorder, a keyboard, a drum machine, and a guitar to produce his first professional recordings.

He contributed tunes to the film soundtracks of *Suburbia* (1997) and *A Life Less Ordinary* (1997).

Benson, top

Ray Benson

Asleep at the Wheel

Born: March 16, 1951 —
Philadelphia, PA

Talent: Guitarist/vocalist

The Road to Fame: Two years after forming the Western Swing Revival band Asleep at the Wheel, Ray and his group became a mainstay of the Berkeley country scene and soon captured the attention of United Artists Records. An unsuccessful debut in 1973 led to lineup changes and label switching until 1975, when they broke through with *Texas Gold*. The group went on to dominate the country charts for the remainder of the decade but hit hard times in the early 1980s. After a brief stint as a producer of solo artists, Ray again reformed the band and released 1987's *10*, an astonishing comeback album. Once again at the top of their game, the group continued its success well into the 1990s.

The Music: **Hit Albums:** *Wheelin' and Dealin'* (1976), *Collision Course* (1978), *Framed* (1980), *Western Standard Time* (1988), *Keepin' Me Up Nights* (1990), *Tribute to the Music of Bob Wills and the Texas Playboys* (1993), *Ride with Bob* (1999)

Hit Singles: "The Letter That Johnny Walker Read" (1975), "House of Blue Lights" (1987), "Way Down Texas Way" (1987), "String of Pars" (1987), "Sugar Foot Rag" (1988)

Did you know? During his hiatus in the mid-1980s, Ray produced records by Aaron Neville, Rob Wasserman, Willie Nelson, and Bruce Hornsby.

The group won Grammys for "String of Pars" and "Sugar Foot Rag" in 1988.

Country legends Merle Haggard, Willie Nelson, Chet Atkins, Brooks & Dunn, Dolly Parton, and Garth Brooks guested on *Tribute to the Music of Bob Wills and the Texas Playboys*.

Eric Bloom
Blue Öyster Cult

Born: December 11, 1944 — Long Island, NY

Talent: Singer/guitarist

The Road to Fame: In 1968, Elektra Records signed the Soft White Underbelly, a psychedelic rock band from New York State. When it came time to buy equipment with their advance money from the label, the SWU members used to frequent the Sam Ash music store where Bloom worked. Eventually, Bloom struck up a friendship with the fledgling band. In 1969, SWU had an acrimonious split with singer Les Braunstein and offered the job to Bloom. The following year, band mentor Sandy Pearlman changed the group's name to the Stalk-Forest Group, and later, to Blue Öyster Cult. Thinking they had the American answer to England's Black Sabbath, Columbia Records signed the band in 1970, releasing BÖC's idiosyncratic yet influential metal records, whose lyrical content leaned heavily on science-fiction and macabre themes.

The Music: Suggested Listening: *Tyranny and Mutation* (1973), *Secret Treaties* (1974), *Agents of Fortune* (1976), *Spectres* (1977)

Did you know? A science-fiction enthusiast, Bloom had enlisted the talents of sci-fi writers like Michael Moorcock to assist in the writing of BÖC song lyrics.

On the early BÖC recordings, Bloom is credited with "stun guitar." The term was just another "cosmic manifestation" out of then-manager Sandy Pearlman's brain. Pearlman tried to generate a stage name for Bloom as he had for guitarist Donald Raeser (aka Buck Dharma), but Bloom would not allow it.

BÖC were one of the first groups to incorporate laser light technology into their live shows.

rbAlpertJudahBauerBeastieBoys Beck RayBenson ERICBLOO
mmyDavisJr. NEIL DIAMOND AdamDurwitz Bob Dylan 9
asonFinn AlanFreed MartyFriedman JUSTINEFRISCHMANN Ke
eterGreen BrettGurewitz RICHARDHELL GregHetson Peter Hi
veKatz LennyKaye CaroleKing MarkKnopfler ALKoo
aLoeb CourtneyLove GARY LUCAS Mamasand the Pap
nfredMann Malcolm McClaren MC SEARCH NateMendel Be
phenPerkins MoniquePowell Phranc JoeyRamone LouRee
e Simmons CARLYSIMON PaulSimon Slash Hillel SlovakDee

Michael Bloomfield

Born: July 28, 1943 — Chicago, IL

Died: February 15, 1981 — San Francisco, CA

Talent: Singer/guitarist

The Road to Fame: Just a year after picking up the guitar, the fourteen-year-old Michael was jamming with the pros at black blues clubs around Chicago. In 1965, following years of session work and a brief contract with Columbia, he was recruited by the Paul Butterfield Blues Band. After two years of recording and touring with the group, as well as recording and performing occasionally with Bob Dylan, Michael formed the short-lived band the Electric Flag. Throughout the 1970s, he remained in San Francisco, gigging with various friends and recording occasional solo projects. Toward the end of the decade, he descended into drug abuse, overdosing fatally in 1981.

The Music: **Landmark Recordings:** "Like a Rolling Stone" (1965, Bob Dylan), *Highway 61 Revisited* (1965, Bob Dylan), *East-West* (1966, Paul Butterfield Blues Band), *Super Session* (1969, with Stephen Stills and Al Kooper)

Did you know? As a fourteen-year-old, Michael was known to join his blues idols onstage and begin jamming with them without asking permission.

He was Dylan's backing guitarist at the infamous 1965 Newport Folk Festival when the folk icon went electric for the first time.

Michael considered the *Super Session* album with Kooper and Stills to be an overly commercial sellout.

Exactly three months before his death, Michael performed "Like a Rolling Stone" onstage with Bob Dylan.

Marc Bolan

T. Rex

Born: Mark Feld, September 30, 1947—London, England

Died: September 16, 1977—London, England

Talent: Singer/songwriter/guitarist

The Road to Fame: Marc and percussionist Steve Peregrine Took formed the acoustic duo Tyrannosaurus Rex in 1967. Three albums later, Marc teamed up with Mickey Finn and scored the first of many U.K. hit singles with "Ride a White Swan" (1970). Expanding into a full-fledged glam-rock band known as T. Rex, Marc and company racked up hit after hit in Great Britain until their popularity began to decline in 1974. Three years later, in the midst of making a comeback touring and recording with T. Rex, Marc was killed in a car accident.

The Music: Landmark Album: *Electric Warrior* (1971)

U.K. Hits: "Children of Rarn" (1970),"Hot Love" (1972), "Telegram Sam" (1972), "Metal Guru" (1972), "The Groover" (1973)

Did you know? As a youth, Marc claimed to have been stabbed in a knife fight while a member of a gang known as "the Sharks."

Marc was considered a hero figure in Britain's punk circles by showing support to such bands as the Damned and the Sex Pistols.

Michael Bolton

Born: Michael Bolotin, February 26, 1954—New Haven, CT

Talent: Singer/songwriter

The Road to Fame: Michael's professional career began in his early twenties with two little-known RCA releases. After recording two more albums with the heavy-metal band Blackjack, he changed his last name to Bolton, signed with Columbia Records, and focused his songwriting on love songs. The success of his self-titled debut in 1983—which earned him songwriting gigs for artists like Barbra Streisand, Cher, and Kenny Rogers—paled in comparison to his breakthrough release, *The Hunger* (1987). His 1989 release, *Soul Provider*, upgraded his status to international superstar. All his subsequent releases have gone multiplatinum.

The Music: Albums: *Michael Bolotin* (1975), *Every Day of My Life* (1976), *Michael Bolton* (1983), *Everybody's Crazy* (1985), *The Hunger* (1987), *Soul Provider* (1989), *Time, Love & Tenderness* (1991), *Timeless Classics* (1992), *The Artistry of Michael Bolton* (1993), *The One Thing* (1993), *Said I Loved You (But I Lied)* (1995), *This Is the Time (The Christmas Album)* (1996), *All That Matters* (1997), *My Secret Passion—The Arias* (1998), *Timeless (The Classics), Vol. 2* (1999)

Hit Singles: "Fools Game," "That's What Love Is All About," "How Am I Supposed to Live Without You," "How Can We Be Lovers," "Love Is a Wonderful Thing"

Awards: 1989 Grammy for Best Pop Male Vocal Performance ("How Am I Supposed to Live Without You"); 1992 Grammy for Best Pop Male Vocal Performance ("When a Man Loves a Woman")

Did you know? Michael sang with opera legend Luciano Pavarotti for a Bosnian benefit concert.

His early idols included R&B masters Ray Charles and Otis Redding.

Michael wrote KISS's 1990 hit "Forever" and collaborated with Bob Dylan on "Steel Bars" on the number-one LP *Time, Love & Tenderness*.

Igor Cavalera

Sepultura

Born: Belo Horizonte,
September 4, 1970—Brazil

Talent: Drummer

Cavalera, left

The Road to Fame: Brothers Max and Igor Cavalera formed Sepultura in 1985, in the midst of social and political upheaval in their native country, Brazil. In 1985, the band's debut album, *Morbid Vision/Bestial Devastations*, was released, and soon the death-metal underground was abuzz about the band. After the release of their 1990 album, *Schizophrenia*, the band decided to relocate to the U.S., choosing Phoenix, Arizona, as a base of operations. Sepultura's love of blistering punk and classic British heavy metal appealed to many in the underground hard rock scene, and with help from legendary death-metal producer Scott Burns and high profile tours opening for Ozzy Osbourne, the band's reputation was cemented. In 1997, however, Igor demanded that Max discharge his wife Gloria from her role as Sepultura's manager. Max quit the band and formed Soulfly, while Igor carried on with the Sepultura name.

The Music: Suggested Listening: *Beneath the Remains* (1989), *Arise* (1991), *Roots* (1996)

Did you know? "Sepultura" is the Portuguese term for "grave."

Igor Cavalera converted to Judaism in 1966 when he married his wife. "I have always had a strong belief in God, and it was very easy for me to accept and learn more about the faith," he says. "The kind of music we play is embraced by young people, teenagers who are rebelling against anything, families, religion, or whatever. At that part of your life, you aren't really going deep inside yourself. Later on in life, you find out about these things and make your own decisions."

10

Leonard Cohen

Born: September 21, 1934—Montreal, Quebec, Canada

Talent: Singer/songwriter/novelist/poet

The Road to Fame: Two years after picking up the guitar, Leonard began singing in cafés around Montreal. Following his earning a bachelor's degree in English from McGill University, he quickly became a well-established poet and novelist. It wasn't until Leonard reached his mid-thirties that folk singer Judy Collins—who had recorded a popular version of his teenage song "Suzanne"—convinced him to consider a future in music. The success of his debut at the 1967 Newport Folk Festival led to his signing with Columbia Records. Though his ensuing 1970s and early 1980s albums were consistently successful, none matched the popularity of 1988's *I'm Your Man*, considered to be his defining musical achievement.

The Music: **Assorted Albums:** *The Songs of Leonard Cohen* (1968), *New Skin for Old Ceremony* (1974), *Recent Songs* (1979), *I'm Your Man* (1988), *The Future* (1992)

Cohen Classics: "Suzanne," "So Long, Marianne," "Bird on a Wire," "First We Take Manhattan," "Ain't No Cure for Love," "Tower of Song"

Did you know? *Let Us Compare Mythologies*, Leonard's first collection of poetry, was published while he was still attending college in 1956.

He once called his collaboration with producer Phil Spector on 1977's *Death of a Ladies' Man* "a catastrophe."

Each of his two novels, *The Favorite Game* (1963) and *Beautiful Losers* (1966), has sold over 800,000 copies worldwide.

Leonard wrote the soundtrack to legendary director Robert Altman's *McCabe and Mrs. Miller* (1971).

He was childhood friends with Jewish actor William Shatner of *Star Trek* fame.

Sammy Davis, Jr.

Born: December 8, 1925—New York (Harlem), NY

Died: May 16, 1990—Beverly Hills, CA

Talent: Singer/actor/tap dancer

The Road to Fame: The son of a chorus girl and a vaudeville performer, Sammy was only six when he joined his father as a singer and dancer in the group Will Mastin's Gang. After serving in the army, Sammy returned to singing with his father and Mastin in 1946, greatly increasing their popularity with the addition of his comic impersonations. A number of high-profile appearances and the influence of his friend Frank Sinatra earned Sammy a recording contract in 1954. Shortly after the release of his debut album, he lost his left eye in a car accident. Sammy quickly recovered, converted to Judaism, and returned triumphantly to the airwaves in 1955 with a number of hit singles like "Something's Gotta Give." After tackling Broadway and film roles in the late 1950s, Sammy formed the fabled Rat Pack with Sinatra, Dean Martin, Peter Lawford, and Joey Bishop at the Sands Casino in Las Vegas. Though Sammy's star continued to rise worldwide as Rat Pack films were released, a portion of the black community considered him a sellout for his participation in a group some considered subtly racist, his conversion to Judaism, and his marriage to a white woman. Despite the controversy, Sammy continued to work with ease, returning to Broadway, continuing his film career with *A Man Called Adam*, and expanding into TV. His number-one hit "The Candy Man" (1971) was followed by a TV variety show and a steady Vegas singing career until the late 1980s. After a final and acclaimed role in the film *Tap*, Sammy died of lung cancer in 1990.

The Music: **More Sammy Hits**: "Love Me or Leave Me," "That Old Black Magic," "Too Close for Comfort," "What Kind of Fool Am I?"

Acclaimed Films: *Anna Lucasta* (1958), *Porgy and Bess* (1959), *Salt and Pepper* (1968), *Sweet Charity* (1969), *One More Time* (1970)

Did you know? Actor Mickey Rooney first suggested that Sammy include his comic impersonations in Will Mastin's Gang.

Sammy made his film debut at age seven in *Rufus Jones for President*, a famous musical short.

Sammy's classic song "Mr. Bojangles" refers to Bill "Bojangles" Robinson, his celebrated tap-dancing teacher.

Sammy faced rampant racism in the military—he was forced to repeat basic training eight times.

He starred in *Mr. Wonderful*, his Broadway debut, for 400 shows.

A photo of Sammy hugging President Richard Nixon in 1973—taken during a gala held in honor of American POWs recently released from Vietnam— enraged many of his Hollywood friends and expanded his rift with the black community.

Neil Diamond

Born: January 24, 1941 — Brooklyn, NY

Talent: Singer/songwriter

The Road to Fame: Neil first ventured into music upon receiving a guitar for his sixteenth birthday. Songwriting became his passion from high school through college at New York University, where he was in pre-med. Taking a songwriting job with a music publisher, Neil dropped out of college just short of graduation and signed with Bang Records in 1966. His first three singles, including "Cherry, Cherry," became Top Ten hits with "I'm a Believer," recorded by the Monkees, a number-one sensation. Neil's popularity as a live solo performer grew during the early 1970s and led to a 1973 contract with Columbia Records. After *Beautiful Noise* became his first platinum LP in 1976, his career exploded, landing him TV specials, sellout tours, and more platinum albums. In 1980, Neil starred in and wrote the soundtrack for *The Jazz Singer*, a remake of the film that had starred his idol, Al Jolson. He continued to record and tour extensively through the 1980s and 1990s with ongoing success as a pop icon.

The Music: **Hits Sampler**: "Girl, You'll Be a Woman Soon," "Sweet Caroline," "Holly Holy," "Cracklin' Rose," "America," "Heartlight," "Hello Again," "The Best Years of Our Lives"

Latest Release: *As Time Goes By: The Movie Album* (1998), an album of movie music themes.

Did you know? Neil's record sales total more than 110 million copies worldwide.

His two-year "Love in the Round" tour featured a 360-degree rotating stage at every concert.

Neil co-starred with screen legend Sir Lawrence Olivier in *The Jazz Singer*.

He recorded the 1978 number-one hit "You Don't Bring Me Flowers" with Barbra Streisand.

Neil paid tribute to 1950s and 1960s pop writing teams like Goffin & King, Mann & Weill, and Leiber & Stoller with *Up on the Roof — Songs from the Brill Building* (1993).

Adam Duritz

Counting Crows

Born: August 1, 1964—Baltimore, MD

Talent: Vocalist/pianist/harmonica player

Duritz, upper right

The Road to Fame: Shortly after Adam and guitarist David Bryson initially hooked up as an acoustic duo in 1991, they recruited keyboard player Charlie Gillingham, drummer Steve Bowman, and bassist Matt Malley to form Counting Crows. Their signing with Geffen Records in 1992 led to a gig at the 1993 Rock and Roll Hall of Fame induction ceremony, where they filled in for their idol, Van Morrison. With the 1994 release of their debut album, *August and Everything After*, the dreadlocked lead singer and his bandmates became MTV darlings and immediately achieved international success. Adam and Counting Crows released their smash-hit follow-up LP, *Recovering the Satellites*, in 1996. A live album was released in 1999.

The Music: Albums: *August and Everything After* (1993), *Recovering the Satellites* (1996), *Across a Wire: Live in NY* (1998), *This Desert Life* (1997)

Breakthrough Hits: "Mr. Jones," "Round Here"

Did you know? Adam dropped out of college two credits short of his bachelor's degree in English.

In the midst of the release of his band's successful debut album, Adam moved to Los Angeles and tended bar to help him deal with his newfound fame.

Bob Dylan

Born: Robert Allen Zimmerman,
May 24, 1941—Duluth, MN

Talent: Singer/songwriter/guitarist

The Road to Fame: Following his graduation from the University of Minnesota in 1959, Zimmerman became a fixture at coffeehouses as a folk singer and dubbed himself Bob Dylan. Bob relocated to New York City in 1961 and garnered attention as an opening act for bluesman John Lee Hooker. Signing with Columbia, he put out an eponymous album that was comprised mostly of covers. It was after the 1962 release of his second album, *The Freewheelin' Bob Dylan*, that his legend was born. Folk acts such as Peter, Paul, & Mary and Joan Baez began to cover and popularize his songs. In 1965, Bob entered the rock-and-roll arena with the hit "Like a Rolling Stone," much to the chagrin of folk devotees. His songs continued to trumpet socialist and transcendental themes and to extol the use of certain drugs, as in "Rainy Day Women No. 12 and 35 (Everybody Must Get Stoned)." He toured and recorded tirelessly for the next thirty years, during which time he explored various religions outside of Judaism, to which he ultimately returned. In 1998, Bob won three Grammys for his 1997 release *Time Out of Mind*.

Bob on Judaism: "My so-called Jewish roots are in Egypt. They went down there with Joseph, and they came back with Moses, you know, the guy that killed the Egyptian, married an Ethiopian girl, and brought the law down from the mountain."

—*City Pages*, 1983

The Music: Assorted Albums: *The Freewheelin' Bob Dylan* (1963), *Highway 61 Revisited* (1965), *New Morning* (1970), *Blood on the Tracks* (1975), *Empire Burlesque* (1985), *Time Out of Mind* (1997)

More Dylan Classics: "Blowin' in the Wind," "The Times They Are a Changin'," "Mr. Tambourine Man," "Knockin' on Heaven's Door"

Famous Tours: 1975: The Rolling Thunder Revue with Joan Baez, Joni Mitchell, Jack Elliot, Arlo Guthrie, Mick Ronson, Roger McGuinn, and Allen Ginsberg.

1986: with Tom Petty and the Heartbreakers

1987: with the Grateful Dead as his backing band

1988–1996: The Never Ending Tour

Did you know? Bob took his adopted last name from poet Dylan Thomas.

He was bar mitzvahed in 1954.

Bob was nearly booed off the stage at the Newport Folk Festival in 1965 when he plugged in an electric guitar.

Bob was involved with the Lubavitch movement in Jerusalem in 1984.

He studied with a rabbi in New York during the early 1970s.

oomfield MarcBolan MICHAELBoltonIgorCavaleraLEONARD COI
n dannyelfman DONALDFAGEN PerryFarrellNickFeldman DougFeig
rt Garfunkel AdamGaynor GerryGoffin NINAGORDO
SusannaHoffs ScottIan Billy JOEL MickJONES Ira Kapla
nyKRAVITZ GettyLee JerryLeiber & Mike Stoller KEITHLev.
rry Manilow DickManitoba BarryMANN Cynthia WI
dler KeithMORRIS Randy Newman NOFX LauraNYRO PHILOC
hanRichman DavidLeeRoth ADAMSANDLER NeilSEDAKA JoSh Silv
illSchule PhilSpector PaulStanley ChrisSTEIN STEVESTEV

Jakob Dylan

The Wallflowers

Born: December 9, 1969

Talent: Singer/songwriter

The Road to Fame: The son of the legendary Bob Dylan, Jakob learned to play guitar at age thirteen and formed the Wallflowers in 1990. When the band's critically acclaimed Virgin Records debut in 1992 failed to sell well, he and keyboardist Rami Jaffee recruited three new bandmates and recorded a new album for Interscope, *Bringing Down the Horse* (1996), which climbed to the top of the charts.

The Music: Breakthrough Hits: "6th Avenue Heartache," "One Headlight"

Did you know? Jakob turned down director John Woo's offer to star in his film *Face/Off* opposite actor Nicholas Cage.

Singers Michael Penn, Sam Phillips, Adam Duritz (Counting Crows), Gary Louris (the Jayhawks), and Tom Petty make guest appearances on *Bringing Down the Horse*.

The Wallflowers played some of their first gigs in the reception room of an L.A. deli.

The group toured with 10,000 Maniacs, the Spin Doctors, Cracker, and Toad the Wet Sprocket in support of their first album.

"When I first started my group, four of the five of us were Jewish. We never discussed it as an advantage or disadvantage. During the fifties, it would have been different. Rock n' Roll exploded from the south; it was in fact dangerous, and northern parents had good reason to be scared. Early on Jews did occupy key roles, only behind the scenes. Leiber and Stoller wrote 'Hound Dog' near the birth of rock, and Brian Epstein managed the Beatles. As performers, Jews were professional, like Paul Simon and Neil Diamond. Maybe great artists, but not the lethal combination that would eventually become the image of rock. Even though it may have been inevitable for Jews to invade all areas of rock, maybe it took the guts of one Jewish kid from Minnesota to stick the smug face of Brando to the ferocious danger of the faraway south. So the rest of us today don't have to consider it a factor at all."—Jakob Dylan

Danny Elfman

Born: May 29, 1953—Amarillo, TX

Talent: Guitarist/keyboardist/film score composer

The Road to Fame: Elfman led the high-spirited L.A.-based octet Oingo Boingo through of mad musical calisthenics for over a decade. Despite an appearance in the 1981 alt-rock precursor film, *URGH! A Music War,* and a spot on the soundtrack of a hit movie (1985's *Weird Science*), the band made little headway outside California. Since Boingo's breakup in 1995, Elfman has been Hollywood's film scorer of choice, respected for his ability to complement visuals in his own inimitable way.

The Music: Recommended Listening: **With Oingo Boingo:** *Only a Lad* (1981), *Nothing to Fear* (1982), *Dead Man's Party* (1985); **Solo:** *Music for a Darkened Theater* (1990)

Film Scores: *Pee Wee's Big Adventure* (1985), *Beetlejuice* (1988), *Batman* (1989), *Edward Scissorhands* (1990), *The Nightmare Before Christmas* (1993), *Scream 2* (1997), *Sleepy Hollow* (1999)

Did you know? Elfman has supplied musical scores to the Fox network animated comedy show, *The Simpsons.*

Television star Jenna Elfman is married to Bodhi Elfman. Bodhi is the son of Danny's older brother, Richard (who was a member of the original Mystic Knights of the Oingo Boingo lineup).

Cass Elliot, John Phillips, and Michelle Phillips

John, second from left;
Michelle, second from right; Cass, right

The Mamas & the Papas

Born: "Mama" Cass Elliot (aka Ellen Naomi Cohen): September 19, 1941—Baltimore, MD; **"Papa" John Phillips:** August 30, 1935—Paris Island, SC; **Michelle Phillips:** April 6, 1944—Long Beach, CA

Died: Cass Elliot: July 29, 1974—London, England

Talent: **Cass:** Singer/songwriter; **John:** Singer/guitarist/songwriter/producer; **Michelle:** Singer

The Road to Fame: In 1964, folk rocker John Phillips formed the Mamas & the Papas in New York with his ex-model wife Michelle and folk veterans Cass Elliot and Denny Doherty. Upon relocating to California the vocal band was signed and became one of the most successful folk acts of their generation, recording numerous hits and garnering attention for their carefree lifestyles. Drug abuse and skewed relationships within the band led to their breakup in 1971. Having separated from Michelle, John went on to become a producer. Cass became a successful solo artist and television personality until she died of heart failure in 1974. The band was inducted into the Rock and Roll Hall of Fame in 1998.

The Music: **Family Hits**: "California Dreaming," "Dedicated to the One I Love," "Go Where I Wanna Go," "Monday, Monday," "Trip, Tumble and Fall," "Got a Feelin'," "Straight Shooter"

Mama's Solo Hits: "Dream a Little Dream of Me," "Make Your Own Kind of Music"

Did you know? Before joining the Mamas & the Papas, Cass was a member of the folk trio the Big Three and the Mugwumps, which included Zal Yanovsky, future member of the Lovin' Spoonful.

Both John and Michelle have written books detailing their lives during the days of the band. To this day, John refuses to speak to Michelle.

Donald Fagen and Walter Becker

Steely Dan

Born: Donald Fagen: January 10, 1948—Passaic, NJ
Walter Becker: February 20, 1950—New York, NY

Becker, top row left; Fagen, top row right

Talent: Donald: Songwriter/keyboardist/vocalist
Walter: Songwriter/guitarist/bassist/producer

The Road to Fame: In 1967, while both attending Bard College in upstate New York, Donald and Walter became friends and songwriting partners. Two years later, they were writing for the vocal group Jay & the Americans, subsequently joining them on a tour. The two signed a contract with ABC Dunhill Records in 1971, and working with various session musicians, they released the jazz-pop LP *Can't Buy a Thrill* the following year. Donald and Walter constantly updated Steely Dan with new musicians throughout their seven albums and world tours until their breakup in 1980. Donald went on to release the hit album *Nightfly*, while Walter became a part-time producer. After producing Donald's *Kamakiriad* in 1993, Walter and his former bandmate set off on a blockbuster Steely Dan reunion tour. A 1995 live album followed after the release of Becker's solo album, *11 Tracks of Whack*, as well as a new album, *Two Against Nature*, in 2000.

The Music: Albums: *Countdown to Ecstasy* (1973), *Pretzel Logic* (1974), *Katy Lied* (1975), *The Royal Scam* (1976), *Aja* (1977), *Gaucho* (1980)

Did you know? Just after leaving college, Donald and Walter tried unsuccessfully to sell their songs to various publishers at the legendary Brill Building.

After the 1980 breakup, Walter moved to Hawaii and became an avocado rancher.

Donald has penned songs for a variety of artists including Diana Ross, the Manhattan Transfer, Jennifer Warnes, and the Yellowjackets.

Walter has produced albums for China Crisis, Rickie Lee Jones, and various jazz artists.

Perry Farrell

Jane's Addiction and Porno for Pyros

Born: Peretz Bernstein, March 29, 1959—Queens, NY

Talent: Singer/songwriter

The Road to Fame: After a brief career as a rock star–impersonating stripper in Newport Beach, California, Perry became the lead singer of the experimental rock band Psi Com. The band gained a loyal following, but fizzled out in 1985, about the time that Perry met bassist Eric Avery. The two began writing songs, and soon formed Jane's Addiction with drummer Stephen Perkins and guitarist Dave Navarro. The band's debut—a self-titled live album released by the L.A.-based indie Triple X—started a bidding war that landed them a deal with Warner Brothers. Their proper studio debut, *Nothing's Shocking* (1988), featured such underground classics as "Mountain Song" and "Jane Says." Their next album, *Ritual de lo Habitual* (1990), was a smash hit, due in part to the single "Been Caught Stealing," an MTV favorite. After the 1991 Lollapalooza tour, which Perry created, the band broke up. The following year, Perry and Steve went on to form Porno for Pyros, whose success nearly equaled that of their previous band.

The Music: More of Perry's Hits: **With Jane's Addiction**: "Mountain Song"; **With Porno for Pyros**: "Freeway," "Hard Charger"

Did you know? Perry shared a house with college football players when he arrived in California.

The name "Jane's Addiction" refers to a junkie friend of Perry and Stephen who was also a prostitute.

Many stores refused to carry the album *Nothing's Shocking* because of the nude sculpture of Perry's girlfriend that graced the cover. He created a papier-mâché "three-way" for the cover of *Ritual* that forced Warner to issue a censored cover for sensitive retailers.

Perry was once arrested for singing nude onstage with Jane's Addiction

Jane's Addiction reunited in 1997, with Red Hot Chili Peppers bassist Flea standing in for Avery.

Eric, left; Mike, with umbrella

Fat Mike and Eric Melvin

NOFX

Born: Fat Mike: January 16, 1967—
   Boston, MA

Eric Melvin: July 9, 1966—
   Los Angeles, CA

Talent: Mike: Bassist/lead vocalist/
   songwriter

Eric: Rhythm guitarist/background vocalist

The Road to Fame: Punk rockers Mike and Eric joined forces with gui-tarist/trumpeter El Hefe and drummer Eric Sandin to form NOFX in 1984. Securing a rabid underground following with the release of six albums on Epitaph Records (owned by Bad Religion's Brett Gurewitz) and two on Fat Wreck Chords, the band remained faithful to their cult roots with their rau-cous sound and scathing lyrics. By the mid-1990s, however, they had unwit-tingly entered the mainstream as their sound had become popular.

The Music: Assorted LPs: *S&M Airlines* (1989), *Liberal Animation* (1988), *White Trash, Two Heebs and a Bean* (1992), *I Heard They Suck . . . Live* (1995), *So Long and Thanks for All the Shoes* (1997), *Pump Up the Valuum* (2000)

Radio Friendly?: "Please Play This Song on the Radio," "Kill All the White Men," "The Brews," "Leave It Alone," "Linoleum," "Don't Call Me White"

Did you know? Mike is the owner of the record label Fat Wreck Chords.

Neither Fat Mike nor Eric Melvin were bar mitzvahed.

NOFX have never toured Israel but they swear they will in the near future.

Nick Feldman

Wang Chung

Born: May 1, 1955 — North London, England

Talent: Bassist/songwriter

Feldman, right

The Road to Fame: Nick formed the London-based new wave band Huang Chung with singer/guitarist Jack Hues and drummer Darren Costin in 1979. After their inconsequential 1982 Arista label debut, they changed their name to Wang Chung, signed with Geffen, and scored two U.S. hits off their second album, *Points on the Curve*, in 1984. Costin left the band just before their next release, which proved to be their biggest ever. Two years after releasing another, less successful LP in 1989, Feldman and Hues disbanded. In 1997 they reunited to record new tracks for a greatest hits CD.

The Music: Albums: *Huang Chung* (1982), *Points on the Curve* (1984), *Mosaic* (1986), *The Warmer Side of Cool* (1989)

Hit singles: "Dance Hall Days," "Don't Let Go," "Let's Go!", "Everybody Have Fun Tonight," "Praying to a New God"

Did you know? Wang Chung wrote the title theme for director William Friedkin's 1985 thriller, *To Live and Die in L.A.*

bAlpertJudahBauerBeastieBoys Beck RayBenson ERICBLOOM
mmyDavisJr. NEIL DIAMOND AdamDurwitz Bob Dylan Jac
sonFinn AlanFreed MartyFriedman JUSTINEFRISCHMANN Ken
terGreen BrettGurewitz RICHARDHELL GregHetson Peter Hir
veKatz LenNYKaye CaroLeKing MarkKnopfler ALKoop
Loeb CourtneyLove GARY LUCAS Mamas and the Papa
nfredMann Malcolm McClaren MC SEARCH NateMendel Ben
phenPerkins MoniquePowell Phranc JoeyRamone LouReed
e Simmons CARLYSIMON PaulSimon Slash Hillel SlovakDeeS

Doug Fieger

The Knack

Born: August 20, 1952—Detroit, MI

Talent: Singer/songwriter/rhythm guitarist

The Road to Fame: In 1978, Doug formed his pop-rock band the Knack, quickly gaining acceptance from performances on L.A.'s Sunset Strip and signing with Capitol Records a year later. Fueled by the hot single "My Sharona," the band's debut was a smashing success. When the band refused interviews with the press, however, the critics turned against them and panned their second LP. With the resulting decline in popularity, the band decided to split up in 1980. A decade later, they attempted a comeback and became regulars on the L.A. club circuit.

The Music: Albums: *Get the Knack* (1979), . . . *But the Little Girls Understand* (1980), *Round Trip* (1981), *Serious Fun* (1991)

Did you know? During a two-week period in 1978, the Knack jammed with Ray Manzarek of the Doors, Tom Petty, Eddie Money, Stephen Stills, and Bruce Springsteen.

In 1979, *Get the Knack* went platinum in six weeks, the fastest debut to go platinum at that time in history.

Get the Knack was the number-one album in the United States for five weeks and went on to sell over 5 million copies.

The Knack received two 1979 Grammy nominations for their debut album.

Doug's brother was a former legal advisor to Dr. Jack Kevorkian who made an unsuccessful bid for governor of the state of Michigan.

The band toured America in 1998 with Missing Persons founder Terry Bozzio on drums.

Finn, right

Jason Finn
The Presidents of the United States of America
Talent: Drummer

The Road to Fame: During his stint drumming with the band Love Battery in 1991, Jason saw a performance given by the Presidents of the United States of America, a sarcastic punk duo consisting of two-string "basitarist"/lead vocalist Chris Ballew and three-string "guitbassist" Dave Dederer. Jason begged to become their drummer until they finally gave in (two years later). In 1995, Columbia Records rereleased their eponymous indie-label debut. The band released a follow-up, *The Presidents of the United States of America: II*, shortly after their first album went double-platinum in 1996. They broke up a year later.

The Music: Presidential Hits: "Lump," "Kitty," "Peaches"

Did you know? The Presidents of the United States of America played at a 1994 Democratic fund-raiser for President Bill Clinton.

Jason and the band received a 1996 Grammy nomination for Best Alternative Music Performance.

The Presidents' unconventional concert venues have included Pink's Hot Dog Stand in L.A., Mount Rushmore (on Presidents' Day), a flatbed truck in Minneapolis, and a bowling alley in Chicago.

The band recreated the theme to the cartoon *George of the Jungle* for the 1997 live-action hit movie.

The Presidents of the United States of America recently reformed with a smaller name, the Presidents. They finished a new recording, *Freaked Out and Small*, for release in 2000.

Alan Freed

Born: December 15, 1922—
Johnstown, PA

Died: January 20, 1965

Talent: DJ/concert promoter/
musician

The Road to Fame: After leading a high-school jazz band called the Sultans of Swing, Alan developed a passion for radio in college and soon became a DJ, eventually establishing himself in Cleveland. His show in the early 1950s consisted mainly of black rhythm and blues, which he helped popularize with the white teenage audience by dubbing it "rock and roll." The format caught on nationwide, and Alan moved on to New York, where he produced a series of live radio shows that attracted mobs of teenagers. By the late 1950s he was a household name, appearing in films and continuing to sway the charts with his show. In 1959, however, Alan was charged with commercial bribery, becoming a scapegoat for DJs nationwide who had accepted "payola" from record companies in exchange for airplay. His career and finances were ruined as a result of the scandal, but he refused to admit any wrongdoing. Freed died, still protesting his innocence, in 1965.

Alan's Films: *Don't Knock the Rock*; *Rock Around the Clock*; *Mr. Rock'n'Roll*; *Rock, Rock, Rock.*

Did you know? Alan's nickname was "Moondog"; his Cleveland radio show was called *Moondog's Rock'n'Roll Party.*

In 1952, his first live stage show—"Moondog's Coronation Ball"—attracted 25,000 fans and nearly caused a riot.

Alan became one of the first inductees into the Rock and Roll Hall of Fame in 1986.

Marty Friedman

Megadeth

Born: December 8, 1962—
Washington, D.C.

Talent: Guitarist

Friedman, bottom right

The Road to Fame: After a stint as the lead guitarist for the heavy-metal band Hawaii, Marty signed with the virtuoso guitar–oriented label Shrapnel Records in 1987 and formed Cacophony with fellow guitar ace Jason Becker. The two parted ways in 1989 to work on solo projects, and Marty was hired as the lead guitarist of Megadeth a year later. His eclectic guitar style—an amalgamation of Japanese, Middle Eastern, and Indian musical elements mixed with blues, jazz, and straight-ahead thrash—elevated the band's music in the eyes of critics and fans alike and helped to push Megadeth to the cutting edge of the heavy-metal genre.

The Music: Albums with Megadeth: *Rust in Peace* (1990), *Countdown to Extinction* (1992), *Youthanasia* (1994), *Hidden Treasures* (1995), *Cryptic Writings* (1997), *Risk* (1999)

Mega-Singles: "Rust in Peace," "Hangar 18," "Holy Wars," "Symphony of Destruction," "Foreclosure of a Dream"

Did you know? As the son of a U.S. diplomat, Marty lived in various countries as a youth and was greatly influenced by the indigenous music of each.

His second solo album, *Scenes*, was produced by new-age music icon Kitaro.

Justine Frischmann
Elastica

Born: September 16, 1969

Talent: Singer/songwriter/guitarist

The Road to Fame: Justine joined the band Suede while studying architecture at London University in 1989. In 1991, she quit the band and formed Elastica a year later. Their single "Line Up" became a U.K. hit in 1994. It was followed later that year by "Connection," which also became a hit in the United States. The popularity of their 1995 self-titled debut album landed them a spot in that year's Lollapalooza tour. After a lenghty hiatus and some personnel changes, they released their second album, *The Menace*, in 2000.

The Music: **Albums:** *Elastica* (1995), *The Menace* (2000)

Did you know? Elastica had the fastest-selling debut LP in U.K. history.

The band performed under the name "Onk" at their first live performance.

Justine was the longtime paramour of Blur frontman Damon Albarn.

Kenny G

Born: Kenneth Gorelick, July 6, 1956—Seattle, WA

Talent: Saxophonist/composer

The Road to Fame: Kenny's professional career began with a brief stint in Barry White's Love Unlimited Orchestra when he was just seventeen. He went on to earn a degree in accounting from the University of Washington while intensely continuing saxophone practice. After college, he joined keyboardist Jeff Lorber's fusion band in 1982 and subsequently landed a contract with Arista Records. With his 1986 release *Duotones*, Kenny had perfected a pop instrumental style that yielded great success. The album's hit single "Songbird" helped to make it go triple-platinum. His releases have been best-sellers ever since.

The Music: **Best-selling Album**: *Breathless* (1992) sold 8 million copies in the United States alone.

Did you know? Kenny initially failed to make the cut for his high school jazz band.

"Songbird" was written for his then future wife Lyndie Benson.

Kenny has practiced four hours a day for twelve years.

He has worked with Aretha Franklin, Whitney Houston, and Natalie Cole.

Kenny released Christmas albums in 1996 and 1998.

Art Garfunkel

Born: November 5, 1941—Queens, NY

Talent: Singer/guitarist/poet

The Road to Fame: After graduating from college in 1963, Garfunkel rejoined old school pal and music partner Paul Simon, forming the legendary folk duo Simon & Garfunkel. In 1970, after six hit albums, countless hit songs, and four Grammys, the pair went their separate ways. While Simon immediately embarked on his solo career, Art tried his hand at film acting, receiving critical acclaim for his roles. A steady stream of various solo projects throughout the 1970s culminated in a reunion concert in Central Park with Simon in 1981—the largest open-air concert in history. A brief tour ensued, but the two again parted and continued with their own projects. Art's 1980s endeavors included film scoring and poetry in addition to his traditional folk recordings. In 1990, both he and Simon were inducted into the Rock and Roll Hall of Fame. The duo last performed together in 1993, selling out a string of New York concerts.

The Music: Greatest Hits with Paul Simon: "The Sound of Silence" (1965), "Scarborough Fair" (1967), "Mrs. Robinson" (1968), "Bridge over Troubled Water" (1970)

Solo Hits: "All I Know" (1973), "I Only Have Eyes for You" (1975), "Bright Eyes" (1979)

Film Roles: *Catch-22* (1969), *Carnal Knowledge* (1971), *Bad Timing: A Sensual Obsession* (1980)

Did you know? Art met Paul Simon in the fifth grade.

Tom and Jerry, their pre–Simon & Garfunkel duo, scored a moderate hit with "Hey, Schoolgirl" in 1957.

Art earned a BA and a master's in mathematics from Columbia University.

Adam Gaynor

matchbox 20

Born: November 26, 1964

Talent: Guitarist

The Road to Fame: In the early 1990s, Adam was employed at the Criteria Recording Studios in Miami when singer/songwriter Rob Thomas recruited him as the rhythm guitarist/guitar orchestrator for his new band matchbox 20. The group signed with Lava/Atlantic and released *Yourself or Someone Like You* in 1996. A year later, a couple of hot singles had pushed the LP to the upper reaches of the charts.

The Music: **Hit Singles**: "Long Day," "Push"

Did you know? Adam's personal motto is "Inner strength . . . inner peace . . . focus . . . fire."

His major musical influences are the Jackson 5, James Taylor, and George Benson.

Gerry Goffin

Born: February 11, 1939—Queens, NY

Talent: Lyricist/singer

The Road to Fame: As a budding lyricist at Queens College in 1958, Gerry met Carole King, a young composer who soon became his songwriting partner and wife. Working out of the famed Brill Building, the duo became one of the most successful pop songwriting teams in history, pumping out hit after hit for a variety of groups during the early 1960s. While Carole found success as a recording artist after the couple's 1968 breakup, Gerry only briefly became a performer and instead forged songwriting partnerships with various composers. Along with his new role as a producer, Gerry continued to pen hits for rock artists throughout the 1980s and 1990s.

The Music: **King and Goffin Hit Sampler**: "Will You Love Me Tomorrow?" (The Shirelles, 1961), "Take Good Care of My Baby" (Bobby Vee, 1961), "The Loco-Motion" (Little Eva, 1962), "Go Away Little Girl" (Steve Lawrence, 1963), "Up on the Roof" (The Drifters, 1963), "One Fine Day" (The Chiffons, 1963), "I'm into Something Good" (Herman's Hermits, 1964), "Don't Bring Me Down" (The Animals, 1966), "Pleasant Valley Sunday" (The Monkees, 1967)

With Michael Masser: "Theme from Mahogany (Do You Know Where You're Going To?)" (Diana Ross, 1976), "Saving All My Love for You" (Whitney Houston, 1985)

With Barry Goldberg: "I've Got to Use My Imagination" (Gladys Knight and the Pips, 1974)

As Solo Recording Artist: *It Ain't Exactly Entertainment* (1973), *Back Room Blood* (1996)

Did you know? Gerry and Michael Masser received an Oscar nomination for "Theme from Mahogany" in 1976.

Gerry and Michael's "Saving All My Love for You" was Whitney Houston's breakthrough hit.

Gerry produced the seven LPs recorded by the Monkees since 1967.

He was inducted into the Rock and Roll Hall of Fame in 1990.

Nina Gordon

Born: November 14, 1967

Talent: Singer/songwriter/guitarist

The Road to Fame: Shortly after meeting fellow vocalist/guitarist Louise Post, the songwriting duo added bassist Steve Lack and Nina's brother Jim Shapiro on drums to form the pop-punk band Veruca Salt in 1993. The group attracted the attention of record execs after several of their indie-produced songs became popular on college radio. Veruca Salt signed with Geffen, who reissued their 1994 release, *American Thighs*. The single "Seether" immediately rocketed up the charts, granting the band instant MTV exposure. The 1996 release of an EP (the Steve Albini–produced *Blow It Out Your Ass It's Veruca Salt*) followed a tour, and the heavier follow-up LP, *Eight Arms to Hold You*, hit stores a year later. Post and Gordon severed their partnership acrimoniously in 1998 amid stories of creative differences, boyfriend-stealing, and other acts of infidelity. In 2000, Gordon recorded a solo album, *Tonight and the Rest of My Life*.

The Music: Singles: "Number One Blind," "All Hail Me," "Volcano Girls"

Influences: Big Star, My Bloody Valentine, the Pixies

Did you know? Nina met Louise through a mutual friend, film actress Lili Taylor.

Veruca Salt has toured with Hole, P. J. Harvey, Hazel, and the Muffs.

Nina and Louise intended to form an all-girl band until Steve Lack auditioned for the bass slot.

"Veruca Salt" is the name of a character in the movie *Willy Wonka and the Chocolate Factory*.

Albert Judah Bauer Beastie Boys Beck Ray Benson ERIC BLOOM nmy Davis Jr. NEIL DIAMOND Adam Durwitz Bob Dylan Jak soh Finn Alan Freed Marty Friedman JUSTINE FRISCHMANN Ker ter Green Brett Gurewitz RICHARD HELL Greg Hetson Peter Hir ve Katz Lenny Kaye Carole King Mark Knopfler AL Koo Loeb Courtney Love GARY LUCAS Mamas and the Papa nfre Mann Malcolm McClaren MC SEARCH Nate Mendel Bet phen Perkins Monique Powell Phranc Joey Ramone Lou Ree e Simmons CARLY SIMON Paul Simon Slash Hillel Slovak Dees

Green, second from left

Peter Green

Fleetwood Mac

Born: Peter Greenbaum, October 29, 1946—Bethnal Green, London, England

Talent: Guitarist/singer/songwriter

The Road to Fame: Beginning the study of guitar at age ten, Peter found early influences in blues guitarists and old Jewish songs. After paying his dues in various pub bands as both a guitarist and a bassist, he joined John Mayall's Bluesbreakers in 1966 and became good friends with the band's rhythm section, bassist John McVie and drummer Mick Fleetwood. When Peter left the band the following year, he convinced John and Mick to accompany him. With the addition of second guitarist Jeremy Spencer, they formed Peter Green's Fleetwood Mac. For the next three years, they toured constantly and recorded acclaimed albums that solidified Peter's status as a guitar icon. However, his abuse of mind-altering drugs contributed to a deteriorating mental condition that ultimately led to his departure from the band in 1970. He made sporadic solo and guest spot recordings throughout the 1970s and early 1980s before retiring. In 1996, he made a surprise return to the music scene with a European tour and a new album.

The Music: Albums with His Fleetwood Mac: *Peter Green's Fleetwood Mac* (1961), *Mr. Wonderful* (1968), *English Rose* (1969), *Then Play On* (1969), *The End of the Game* (1970), *Live at the Boston Tea Party* (1998)

Memorable Singles: "Black Magic Woman," "Albatross," "Stop Messin' Around," "Need Your Love So Bad," "Green Manalishi (With the Two-Pronged Crown)"

Solo Albums: *In The Skies* (1979), *Little Dreamer* (1980), *White Sky* (1981), *Peter Green Splinter Group* (1997)

Did you know? Peter was hired as the departed Eric Clapton's replacement in John Mayall's Bluesbreakers.

Fans nicknamed him "The Green God."

In the midst of an LSD trip, Peter once proposed that Fleetwood Mac give all their money to charities.

Brett Gurewitz

Bad Religion

Talent: Guitarist/songwriter/
producer/label owner

The Road to Fame: L.A. guitarist Gurewitz formed the hardcore/punk-rock band Bad Religion in 1980 with vocalist Greg Graffin and a rhythm section that would change often during the next decade and a half. Releasing their 1982 debut on Epitaph Records, Brett's own label, the band became a national mainstay of the underground punk movement. In 1984, Brett hired Circle Jerks guitarist Greg Hetson to fill in for him while he received treatment for drug abuse. In 1987 he resumed recording with the band, which remained popular outside the mainstream until 1993, when their album *Recipe for Hate* was considered en vogue. After their first major-label LP was released in 1994, Brett left the band to spend more time with his growing record label.

The Music: Albums: *How the Hell Could It Be Any Worse?* (1982), *Into the Unknown* (1983), *Suffer* (1988), *No Control* (1989), *Against the Grain* (1990), *Generator* (1992), *Recipe for Hate* (1993), *Stranger than Fiction* (1994), *The Gray Race* (1996)

Did you know? Brett's record label, Epitaph, has recorded bands such as the Circle Jerks, NOFX, Pennywise, Rancid, the Offspring, and H20.

Respected singer/songwriter Tom Waits chose to sign with Gurewitz's indie label for his first recordings since leaving Island Records in 1992.

Richard Hell

Born: Richard Myers, October 2, 1949—Lexington, Kentucky

Talent: Singer/songwriter/bassist/actor/novelist

The Road to Fame: In 1971, Hell formed a band called the Neon Boys with his friend Tom Verlaine. In time, the band became Television, one of NYC's highly influential guitar-based new wave rock bands. In 1975, Hell was frustrated with Verlaine's control of the band, so he left Television to form the legendary Heartbreakers with notorious New York Dolls guitarist Johnny Thunders and drummer Jerry Nolan. His tenure with this band was short-lived, and in 1976, Hell put together the Voidoids, a spiky, atonal punk band featuring the talents of drummer Mark Bell and vibrant guitarists Robert Quine and Ivan Julian. The Voidoids didn't last very long after the release of their classic first album, *Blank Generation*; Bell became the Ramones' drummer, and guitarists Quine and Julian did session work. It wasn't until five years later that Hell would resurface with a new album, 1982's *Destiny Street*. After the release, Hell decided to leave music entirely to focus on writing and film work.

The Music: Suggested Listening: *Blank Generation* (1977), *Destiny Street* (1982)

Did you know? Manager Malcolm McLaren—impressed by Hell's look of tattered t-shirts held together with safety pins—begged Hell to move to England to join a band he was putting together called the Sex Pistols. Hell just laughed him off.

Hell appears in the 1988 movie *Desperately Seeking Susan* alongside Madonna and Rosanna Arquette.

In 1993, Hell collaborated with Sonic Youth members Thurston Moore and Steve Shelley and Don Fleming (Gumball) for a short-lived project called Dim Stars.

Hetson, right

Greg Hetson
The Circle Jerks and Bad Religion

Talent: Guitarist

The Road to Fame: Greg, former guitarist of the band Redd Kross, started the hardcore punk band Circle Jerks with ex–Black Flag lead singer Keith Morris in 1979. With the release of their 1980 debut, *Group Sex*, they instantly became punk icons. After two more releases in the early 1980s, the group took a long hiatus, during which Greg joined Bad Religion. He continues to tour and record with the two bands. Ironically, neither of Greg's bands signed with major labels until the 1990s.

The Music: Other Circle Jerks Albums: *Wild in the Streets* (1982), *Golden Shower of Hits* (1983), *Wonderful* (1985), *VI* (1987), *Gig* (1992)

Jerks' AM Radio Hits: "Along Comes Mary," "Afternoon Delight," "Having My Baby," "Love Will Keep Us Together"

Did you know? Before he joined their band in 1984, Greg contributed some guitar tracks to Bad Religion's debut album.

On the Circle Jerks' major-label debut, *Oddities, Abnormalities and Curiosities* (1995), teenybopper Debbie Gibson sang with them on "I Wanna Destroy You," a Soft Boys cover.

Peter Himmelman

Born: Minneapolis, MN

Talent: Singer/songwriter/multi-instrumentalist

The Road to Fame: In the 1970s, Peter led the new wave Sussman Lawrence band as its singer and guitarist. He moved on to folk rock in the mid-1980s and quickly established a signature songwriting style that incorporated Jewish themes, narratives, and mysticism in an effort to bring spirituality to listeners of all faiths.

The Music: Albums: *This Father's Day* (1986), *Gematria* (1987), *Synesthesia* (1989), *Strength to Strength* (1991), *Skin* (1994), *Stage Diving* (1996), *My Best Friend Is a Salamander* (1997)

Did you know? Peter is Bob Dylan's son-in-law.

He has performed Yiddish songs that his grandmother taught him.

Peter produced and performed (vocals, bass, organ, guitar) on a Hanukah album, *Festival of Lights*, in 1996.

He was photographed by the J. Geils Band for their 1974 album *Nightmares*.

He played piano on David Bowie's *Low* (1977).

Susanna Hoffs

The Bangles

Born: January 17, 1961 — Newport Beach, CA

Talent: Singer/guitarist/songwriter

The Road to Fame: In 1981, Susanna joined sisters Debbi and Vicki Peterson and Annette Zilinskas (replaced by Michael Steele in 1984) to become the lead vocalist and rhythm guitarist for the Bangles. After transforming their edgy garage-band sound into a more pop-oriented vibe, they landed a contract with Columbia in 1983. Their debut LP, *All Over the Place*, established them as a competent ensemble, but it was their next album, 1986's *Different Light*, that popularized the band with the aid of several hit singles. Though the subsequent *Everything* (1988) proved successful, the band could not overcome its internal turmoil and broke apart. Susanna, who had become the most recognizable Bangle, moved on to a solo career.

The Music: Hit Singles: "Manic Monday" (written by Prince), "Walk Like an Egyptian," "Hazy Shade of Winter" (written by Simon & Garfunkel), "Eternal Flame," "My Side of the Bed" (solo)

Solo Albums: *When You're a Boy* (1991), *Susanna Hoffs* (1996)

Did you know? Susanna drew criticism from her bandmates after appearing in the steamy B-movie *The Allnighter*.

She is married to *Austin Powers* director Jay Roach.

Susanna's first solo album featured songs written by Cyndi Lauper, Juliana Hatfield, and Diane Warren.

Scott Ian

Anthrax

Born: Scott Rosenfeld, December 31, 1963—Queens, NY

Talent: Guitarist/songwriter

The Road to Fame: Scott formed the New York–based speed-metal band Anthrax in 1981, becoming their primary songwriter and second guitarist, opposite lead thrasher Danny Spitz. With the band's popularity surging in the later half of the 1980s, Anthrax had reached the league of such legends as Megadeth and Metallica. By the 1990s Anthrax was setting heavy-metal trends with their baseball caps, surfer clothes, the introduction of rap into their music, and their silly stage antics. Through the years, Scott successfully kept the band together, enabling them to survive various shakeups including the departure of two lead singers and Spitz's ultimate resignation in 1995.

The Music: Breakthrough Release: *Spreading the Disease* (1985)

Heavy Hits: "Anti-Social," "Indians," "I Am the Law," "Make Me Laugh," and a cover of Joe Jackson's "Got the Time"

Into the Mainstream: *State of Euphoria* (1988), *Persistence of Time* (1990), *Attack of the Killer B's* (1991), *Sound of White Noise* (1993), *Stomp 442* (1995), *Volume 8: The Threat Is Real* (1998)

Classic Collaboration: In 1989, the band joined militant rappers Public Enemy for a cover of PE's "Bring the Noise."

Did you know? Scott Ian and Charlie Benante (Anthrax) formed a side project called S.O.D. (Stormtroopers of Death).

Billy Joel

Born: William Joseph Martin Joel, May 9, 1949—Hicksville, Long Island, NY

Talent: Singer/songwriter/pianist/composer

The Road to Fame: Beginning piano study at age four, Billy worked his way through a series of rock bands during his teenage years. In 1968, his band the Hassles was signed by United Artists. After two unsuccessful albums with that band, Billy began his solo career in 1971. The 1974 release of *Piano Man* made him a superstar. Fifteen albums later, Billy Joel remains one of the industry's most popular and honored musicians. Recently, he has decided to pursue avenues other than rock, including classical music composition.

The Music: Albums: *Piano Man* (1973) *The Stranger* (1977), *Glass Houses* (1980), *An Innocent Man* (1983), *Storm Front* (1989), *River of Dreams* (1993)

Greatest Hits: "New York State of Mind," "Uptown Girl," "Piano Man," "An Innocent Man," "A Matter of Trust," "We Didn't Start the Fire"

> **DYLAN ON JOEL:**
> "To have a great artist like Billy Joel record a song of mine ['To Make You Feel My Love'] is indeed an honor."

Did you know? Billy was a teenage member of a street gang and fought twenty-two bouts as a boxer before devoting all of his time to the piano.

His first solo album, *Cold Spring Harbor*, was mastered at the wrong speed.

"Piano Man" was inspired by Billy's performances at two L.A. piano bars in which he used the stage name "Billy Martin."

Billy has sold more than 90 million albums worldwide (63 million of those in the United States).

Billy has won five Grammys, the Grammy Legend Award, the ASCAP Founders Award, and a place in the Songwriter's Hall of Fame.

He was the first American rock star to tour the Soviet Union, in 1987.

Mick Jones

The Clash and Big Audio Dynamite

Born: June 26, 1955 — Brixton, England

Talent: Guitarist/songwriter

The Road to Fame: Mick formed the Clash in 1976 with members of his previous punk band, the London SS, including vocalist/rhythm guitarist Joe Strummer. After signing with CBS Records, they released their angry self-titled debut the following year, receiving enormous acclaim. Mick and Joe expanded the sound of the band by adding elements of reggae, ska, and R&B while cranking out chart-topping hits from the late 1970s until the early 1980s. Following a successful U.S. tour and supporting role in the Who's farewell tour, Mick was fired from the band in 1983 over artistic differences. Two years later, he returned to the music scene with his new band, Big Audio Dynamite, which incorporated elements of funk, sampling techniques, and dance rhythms into its punk roots. Mick revamped B.A.D. in 1991 and saw a substantial increase in commercial success.

The Music: The Clash's Landmark Albums: *The Clash* (1977), *London Calling* (1979), *Combat Rock* (1982)

Clashing Hits: "This Is Radio Clash," "White Riot," "Train in Vain," "Should I Stay or Should I Go?," "Rock the Casbah"

B.A.D. Albums: *This Is Big Audio Dynamite* (1985), *Megatop Phoenix* (1989), *The Globe* (1991), *Higher Power* (1994), *E-Punk* (1995)

B.A.D. Singles: "The Bottom Line," "E=MC^2," "The Globe," "Rush"

Did you know? The Clash headlined the "Rock Against Racism" concert in 1980.

Mick nearly died after contracting chicken pox, which he caught from his daughter in 1988.

Kaplan, left

Ira Kaplan
Yo La Tengo

Talent: Singer/songwriter/guitarist

The Road to Fame: Ira and his wife, drummer Georgia Hubley, formed Yo La Tengo in 1984 out of Hoboken, New Jersey. The band, which combined the proto-punk stylings of the Velvet Underground with pop-rock and experimental influences, became an indie phenomenon upon the release of their 1986 debut LP, *Ride the Tiger*. Braving several lineup changes over the years, Ira and Georgia remain the stable core of the group, while continuing to garner increasing acclaim from critics with each successive album they release.

The Music: **Assorted Albums:** *Ride the Tiger* (1986), *New Wave Hot Dogs* (1987), *President Yo La Tengo* (1989), *May I Sing with Me* (1992), *I Can Hear the Heart Beating as One* (1997)

Random Cuts: "The River of Water," "Barnaby, Hardly Working," "The Evil That Men Do," "Mushroom Cloud of Hiss," "Big Day Coming"

Did you know? The group portrayed the Velvet Underground in the 1996 film *I Shot Andy Warhol*.

"Yo La Tengo" means "I've Got It"—what a Spanish ballplayer would yell to his teammates.

The group publishes *The Yo La Tengo Gazette*, a newsletter dedicated to the band's activities, as well as to their obsession with baseball.

Steve Katz

The Blues Project
and Blood, Sweat &
Tears

Born: May 9, 1945 — Brooklyn, NY

Talent: Guitarist/singer/songwriter

The Road to Fame: In 1965, Steve left the Even Dozen Jug Band to join the Blues Project, a collection of mostly Jewish musicians experimenting with a mixture of blues, jazz, folk, and psychedelia. After three groundbreaking albums and the departure of legendary organist Al Kooper, the band dissolved in 1967. With Kooper, Steve went on to form the rock/jazz fusion ensemble Blood, Sweat & Tears, which featured a horn section. After two albums that relied on vocal-driven rock tunes, Steve and the group began to favor a jazzier direction with their 1970 release and continued on this path until their breakup in 1980.

The Music: Defining Moments with the Blues Project: "Fly Away," "Steve's Song," "No Time Like the Right Time"

Platinum Hits with B, S & T: "You Made Me So Very Happy," "And When I Die," "Spinning Wheel"

Best-Selling Album: *Blood, Sweat & Tears* (1969)

Did you know? Blood, Sweat & Tears' self-titled album made Recording Industry Association of America history as the first time an album contained three million-selling singles.

Katz produced several albums for Lou Reed, including *Rock and Roll Animal* (1974), *Sally Can't Dance* (1974), *Lou Reed Live* (1975), and *Between Thought and Expression* (1996).

In 1977, Katz became East Coast Director of A&R at Mercury Records, and soon became vice president of the label.

After visiting Ireland in the late 1970s, Katz immersed himself in Irish culture, and in 1987 he became the director of Green Linnet, a record label focused on promoting traditional Irish music in America.

Lenny Kaye

Born: New Brunswick, NJ

Talent: Guitarist/songwriter/rock critic/producer

The Road to Fame: After a short stint as a solo recording artist and free-lance rock critic, Lenny met poet/singer Patti Smith in New York in 1972 and the duo began to collaborate on performance poetry and songwriting. In 1973, Lenny became the lead guitarist for the newly formed Patti Smith Group, a proto-punk band that recorded four influential studio albums from 1975 until their breakup in 1979. Lenny continued to perform with the Lenny Kaye Connection and poet Jim Carroll in the early 1980s, but he focused primarily on producing new artists and various rock genre compilations. Additionally, he enjoyed sporadic work as a rock historian and critic. Lenny rejoined Smith as guitarist and producer for her 1996 comeback album, *Gone Again*.

The Music: With Patti Smith: *Horses* (1975), *Radio Ethiopia* (1976), *Easter* (1978), *Wave* (1979), *Gone Again* (1996)

Did you know? Lenny has produced LPs for various artists including Suzanne Vega and Soul Asylum.

In 1986, he taught a popular rock-and-roll history course at his alma mater, Rutgers University, where he had earned his BA and MA in history.

Lenny has regularly contributed articles to *Rolling Stone*, *Creem*, and *Addicted to Noise* (online).

He penned a biography of Waylon Jennings in 1996.

Volman, second from left
Kaylan, third from right

Howard Kaylan and Mark Volman

The Turtles and Flo & Eddie

Born: Howard: Born Howard Kaplan, June 22, 1947 — New York, NY

Mark: April 19, 1947 — Los Angeles, CA

Talent: Howard: Singer/songwriter

Mark: Singer/songwriter

The Road to Fame: Shortly after meeting in high school, Howard and Mark formed the Nightriders in 1961. The band went through a number of lineup, name, and style changes before becoming the Turtles and scoring a hit single with Bob Dylan's "It Ain't Me Babe" in 1965. After recording a steady stream of hits until the Turtles' 1970 dissolution, Howard and Mark became the Phlorescent Leech and Eddie, the comedic frontmen for Frank Zappa's Mothers of Invention. After their departure in 1972, "Flo & Eddie" went on to become both radio personalities and a sought-after backing-vocal duo, recording with various bands in addition to producing their own albums of satirical tunes and song parodies. In the early 1980s, they wrote and recorded TV commercial jingles and cartoon themes before reforming the Turtles in 1982 as a nostalgia act.

The Music: Turtle Hits: "Let Me Be," "You Baby," "Happy Together," "She'd Rather Be with Me," "Elenore"

As Flo & Eddie: *Flo & Eddie* (1973), *Illegal, Immoral and Fattening* (1974)

Did you know? Howard and Mark's idiosyncratic vocals can be heard on records by artists as diverse as Bruce Springsteen, Marc Bolan's T. Rex, and the Psychedelic Furs.

They wrote the screenplay to the 1974 X-rated animated movie *Cheap*.

They wrote and recorded the themes for the children's cartoon series *Strawberry Shortcake* and *The Care Bears*.

Carole King

Born: Carole Klein, February 9, 1942—Brooklyn, NY

Talent: Songwriter/singer

The Road to Fame: Carole delved into music early, beginning piano at age four and forming her first band in high school. While attending Queens College, she performed at rock shows hosted by the legendary DJ Alan Freed and befriended songwriters such as Paul Simon, Neil Sedaka, and Gerry Goffin. Carole later married Goffin and the two became a songwriting team, working out of the famous Brill Building. Beginning with their 1961 hit "Will You Love Me Tomorrow" (recorded by the Shirelles), the duo wrote over one hundred hit songs for performers ranging from the Beatles to Aretha Franklin. After her marriage to Goffin ended, Carole struggled with a solo career that ultimately proved triumphant when her 1971 release, *Tapestry*, became an enduring hit. Continuing to write hit songs through the early 1980s, Carole took a respite from music to become an environmental activist. She returned to the scene in 1993 with *Colour of Your Dreams*.

The Music: Some Notable Hits: "One Fine Day" (recorded by the Chiffons), "Pleasant Valley Sunday" (The Monkees), "Up on the Roof" (The Drifters), "Chains" (The Cookies and the Beatles), "(You Make Me Feel) Like a Natural Woman" (Aretha Franklin)

Did you know? "Loco-Motion," one of Carole's and Gerry Goffin's first hit songs, was recorded by their babysitter, Little Eva.

Tapestry remained on the charts for over six years.

Guitarist Slash appeared on Carole's 1993 release *Colour of Your Dreams*.

Carole has performed and recorded with the likes of B. B. King; the Monkees; James Taylor; Carly Simon; the Everly Brothers; Crosby, Stills & Nash; and Celine Dion.

Mark Knopfler

Dire Straits

Born: August 12, 1949—Glasgow, Scotland

Talent: Guitarist/singer/songwriter/composer

The Road to Fame: After gigging with various pub bands in the early to mid-1970s, Mark formed Dire Straits with brother David (guitar), John Illsley (bass), and Pick Withers (drums) in 1977. The release of their debut album in 1978 yielded an international hit, "Sultans of Swing," and introduced Mark's guitar genius to the world. David departed after the group's second album, and after two more LPs, Dire Straits' sound was dramatically changed with the addition of keyboardist Alan Clark. Their 1985 release, *Brothers in Arms*, was the beginning of a new rockier direction for the band, and proved to be their most successful album. Taking advantage of the fledgling MTV and CD technology, the group broke ground in music promotion and marketing. Mark took a break from the band to record several side projects including *Neck and Neck*, a 1990 LP with the legendary Chet Atkins. After two more albums with Dire Straits, Mark disbanded the group in 1995 and set off on a full-fledged solo career.

The Music: **Dire Hits**: "Sultans of Swing," "Walk of Life," "Money for Nothing," "Industrial Disease"

Film Scores: *Local Hero* (1983), *Cal* (1984), *The Princess Bride* (1987), *Last Exit to Brooklyn* (1989), *Wag the Dog* (1998)

Did you know? Mark named the group Dire Straits after their dismal financial state during the pub band years.

Bob Dylan invited Mark to play with him after hearing Dire Straits' *Communiqué* (1979).

David Knopfler left Dire Straits after Mark criticized him for lack of practice.

Mark has recorded with artists ranging from Bob Dylan, Steely Dan, Thin Lizzy, and Sting to Tina Turner, the Judds, Buddy Guy, and Clint Black.

Al Kooper

The Blues Project and Blood, Sweat & Tears

Born: February 5, 1944—Brooklyn, NY

Talent: Guitarist/organist/songwriter/producer

The Road to Fame: Kooper began his professional career at fifteen as guitarist for the Royal Teens before becoming a freelance session musician/songwriter, penning songs like Gary Lewis and the Playboys' hit, "This Diamond Ring." Ironically, he ended up playing organ—which he hardly knew at the time—on Bob Dylan's "Like a Rolling Stone" (1965). His keyboard skills progressed at an astounding rate, and he soon became the organist and primary songwriter for the Blues Project, which he left in 1967 to form the rock-jazz fusion band Blood, Sweat & Tears with guitarist Steve Katz. After their debut, *Child Is Father to the Man* (1968), he left to release several solo records and to become a respected producer.

The Music: With the Blues Project: *Live at the Cafe Au-Go-Go* (1966), *Projections* (1966), *Live at Town Hall* (1967)

Suggested Solo albums: *You Never Know Who Your Friends Are* (1969), *Al's Big Deal* (1989)

Did you know? Al played organ on four Bob Dylan albums: *Highway 61 Revisited*, *Blonde on Blonde*, *New Morning*, and *Under the Red Sky*.

He had guest guitar spots on the Rolling Stones' *Let It Bleed* and Jimi Hendrix's *Electric Ladyland*.

In 1968, Al recorded a blockbuster jam record, *Super Session*, with Mike Bloomfield and Stephen Stills.

He discovered Lynyrd Skynyrd and produced their first three albums.

In 1998, he wrote a memoir about the music industry titled *Backstage Groupies and Backstabbing Bastards*.

Lenny Kravitz

Born: May 26, 1964—New York City, NY

Talent: Singer/songwriter/guitarist

The Road to Fame: Growing up in New York and Los Angeles, Lenny was exposed to the gamut of musical styles as a youth. From reggae to classical, funk and R&B, to gospel and rock, his influences shined through in his eclectic debut *Let Love Rule* in 1989. His subsequent releases, *Mama Said* (1991) and *Are You Gonna Go My Way* (1993) elevated him to MTV-friendly status, making him one of modern rock's more recognizable faces.

The Music: Recent Releases: *Circus* (1995), *5* (1998)

Hit Singles: "It Ain't Over Til It's Over," "Are You Gonna Go My Way," "Bullet"

Main Influences: Jimi Hendrix, Motown, English rock and roll

Did you know? Lenny is half-Bahamian (mother) and half-Jewish (father).

He is the son of NBC producer Sy Kravitz and actress Roxie Roker, who played Helen on *The Jeffersons*.

As a child in New York, Lenny befriended Duke Ellington.

As an L.A. teen, he joined the California Boys Choir and performed in the Metropolitan Opera.

Lenny attended Beverly Hills High School with fellow half-Jewish rocker Slash.

LENNY'S ULTIMATE GOAL:
"To express myself as purely as possible and to be as close to God as possible."

Krieger, upper right

Robbie Krieger

The Doors

Born: January 8, 1946—Los Angeles, CA

Talent: Guitarist/arranger/bandleader

The Road to Fame: Drummer John Densmore tapped the jazz and flamenco-influenced Krieger to play with him, keyboardist Ray Manzarek, and brooding vocalist Jim Morrison in the Doors. Although the media constantly scrutinized the booze-and-drug-fuelled adventures of the charismatic Morrison during the band's career, critics cited Krieger's interplay with organist Manzarek as a key ingredient to the band's brooding atmospheric sound. After Morrison's death in 1971, the Doors carried on as a trio for two more albums before dissolving in 1973. Densmore and Krieger worked together in the Butts Band for two fairly inconsequential recordings before pursuing other musical avenues. In 1978, the surviving Doors members wrote new music to accompany some unearthed Morrison spoken-word poetry recordings, later released in 1978 as *An American Prayer*.

The Music: Suggested Listening: With the Doors: *The Doors* (1967), *The Soft Parade* (1969), *L.A. Woman* (1971); **Solo:** *Organization* (1995)

Did you know? Krieger studied under master sitar player Ravi Shankar prior to joining the Doors.

Krieger currently plays clubs across America with his repertory group, the Robbie Krieger Band.

The first music Krieger heard and enjoyed was Prokofiev's *Peter and the Wolf*. Krieger was seven at the time.

In his teens, Krieger was a big blues fan. He acknowledges the influence of the Paul Butterfield Blues Band as his impetus for playing rock.

Geddy Lee

Rush

Born: Gary Lee Weinrib, July 29, 1953—Willowdale, Toronto, Canada

Talent: Singer/composer/bassist/keyboardist

The Road to Fame: In 1969, Geddy's wailing vocal abilities and bass heroics earned him the position of lead singer/bassist in Rush, a Toronto-based rock band consisting of guitarist Alex Lifeson and drummer John Rutsey. After releasing a self-titled debut in 1974, Rutsey left the band due to illness and was replaced by super-drummer/lyricist Neil Peart. With his addition the band changed directions, venturing into virtuosic progressive rock. This formula proved successful with their futuristic breakthrough LP, *2112* (1976). Though critics called them pretentious, Rush quickly built a loyal international following and even scored mainstream hits like "Freewill," "Spirit of the Radio," and "Tom Sawyer" in the early 1980s. They continued to release multi-platinum studio and live albums through the 1990s and continue to be one of the world's most popular live acts.

The Music: Hit Records: *Fly by Night* (1975), *2112* (1976), *Permanent Waves* (1980), *Moving Pictures* (1981), *Grace Under Pressure* (1984), *Power Windows* (1985)

Recent Release: The triple-CD live set *Different Stages* (1998)

Did you know? In addition to his vocals, Geddy sometimes plays three instruments at once (bass, keyboard, Taurus pedals) during live shows.

He got his nickname from his grandmother's Yiddish-accented pronunciation of "Gary"—it came out as "Geddy."

Geddy has a great sense of humor: In addition to contributing vocals to the Doug and Bob McKenzie comedy album, *Great White North*, Geddy also appeared on the *South Park: Bigger, Longer, and Uncut* soundtrack album, singing the Canadian national anthem, "O Canada."

Leiber, left; Stoller, right

Jerry Leiber and Mike Stoller

Lieber & Stoller

Born: **Jerry Leiber:** April 25, 1933—Baltimore, MD
Mike Stoller: March 13, 1933—Long Island, NY

Talent: Songwriters/producers

The Road to Fame: Meeting as teens in Los Angeles in 1950, the precocious duo began writing for R&B artists such as Big Joe Turner and Ruth Brown. Shortly after writing the hit "Hound Dog" for Big Mama Thornton in 1953, they formed Spark Records and scored early hits with the Robins (later called the Coasters). Soon bought out by Atlantic Records, Jerry and Mike worked as producers for the label before relocating to the Brill Building in New York. Though they were already firmly established songwriters, Elvis Presley's 1956 recording of "Hound Dog" made them the hottest duo in the industry. While they continued to write for the King and groups like the Drifters and the Coasters, Jerry and Mike became innovative producers, adding such ornaments as Latin rhythms and string sections to hit songs. In 1964, they formed a new label, Red Bird, and produced successful girl groups like the Dixie Cups and the Shangri-Las before selling off the label two years later in order to become freelance producers.

The Music: **Classic Hits**: "Smokey Joe's Café" (The Robins), "Poison Ivy" (The Coasters), "Love Potion Number 9" (The Coasters/The Searchers), "Yakety Yak" (The Coasters), "Charlie Brown" (The Coasters), "Searchin' " (The Coasters), "Love Me Tender" (Elvis Presley), "Jailhouse Rock" (Elvis Presley), "Fools Fall in Love" (Elvis Presley), "On Broadway" (The Drifters), "Save the Last Dance for Me (The Drifters)

Did you know? Jerry and Mike scored the Elvis films *Jailhouse Rock* and *Love Me Tender*.

They collaborated with Brill Building veterans Doc Pomus and Mort Schuman on Elvis's "She's Not You" and the Coasters' "Young Blood."

In 1987, Jerry and Mike were inducted into the Rock and Roll Hall of Fame.

"Hound Dog," which is credited with launching Elvis Presley's career, won them a Grammy Hall of Fame Award in 1988.

The Broadway musical *Smokey Joe's Café* is a review of their works.

Keith Levene

Public Image Ltd.

Born: Mid 1950s—England

Talent: Guitarist

The Road to Fame: A member of Mick Jones's the London SS, Keith went on to join the Clash in 1976, but left shortly after their first few concerts to form Public Image Ltd. (PiL), which was fronted by Johnny Lydon, aka Johnny Rotten of the Sex Pistols. After recording four albums over a five-year period with the band, Keith split from PiL and completed a series of solo EP's.

The Music: Albums with PiL: *Public Image* (1978), *Metal Box* (1979), *Paris Au Printemps* (1980), *The Flowers of Romance* (1981).

Did you know? Members of the Red Hot Chili Peppers, Fishbone, and Thelonious Monster guested on Keith's second EP.

He has kept a low profile since leaving PiL, and was last seen in 1997 working in the studio with original Sex Pistols bassist Glen Matlock.

Lisa Loeb

Born: March 11, 1968—Bethesda, Maryland

Talent: Singer/songwriter

The Road to Fame: After years of piano lessons, parts in local musicals, and music theory study, Lisa picked up the guitar at age fourteen and began writing original songs the following year. After attending Brown University, during which she performed in both an acoustic duo and a rock band, she briefly attended Berklee School of Music and formed the band Nine Stories. In 1992, Lisa and the band toured the Midwest and New York, selling a demo cassette, *The Purple Tape*, to audiences. Shortly after recording the single "Stay (I Missed You)," Lisa's friend, actor Ethan Hawke, convinced *Reality Bites* director Ben Stiller to include the song on the movie's soundtrack. "Stay" became one of the biggest hits of 1994, leading to Lisa's signing with Geffen and the 1995 release of *Tails*. Her 1997 follow-up, *Firecracker*, immediately spawned the Top Forty hit "I Do."

The Music: More Movie Music: "Truthfully" from *One Fine Day*; "How" from *Twister*

Did you know? As a kid, Lisa played Linus in *You're a Good Man Charlie Brown* at the local Jewish Community Center.

Singer Duncan Sheik played guitar in Lisa's college band.

Lisa is the first unsigned recording artist in history to land a number-one hit in the United States.

"Stay" earned Lisa and Nine Stories a 1994 Grammy nomination for Best Pop Performance by a Group. They won a Brit Award for Best International Newcomer.

Lisa has performed with Lyle Lovett, Sarah McLachlan, Counting Crows, Emmylou Harris, Shawn Colvin, and the Indigo Girls.

Courtney Love

Hole

Born: July 9, 1965 — San Francisco, CA

Talent: Singer/songwriter/guitarist

The Road to Fame: After playing in various bands with future members of L7, Babes in Toyland, and Faith No More, Courtney formed Hole in 1989 and debuted with the bombastic *Pretty on the Inside* two years later. One year after her high-profile 1992 marriage to Nirvana's Kurt Cobain, she and the band began work on a new album, *Live Through This*. Shortly before its 1994 release, Cobain committed suicide, devastating Courtney and threatening to end her career. Despite another tragedy—the deadly heroin overdose of bassist Kristen Pfaff—Hole set off on a U.S. tour in support of their new album, which was selling tremendously well. After completing the 1995 Lollapalooza tour, Courtney took a respite from music in order to pursue a promising film career. She later regrouped Hole and completed a third album, *Celebrity Skin* (1998), which featured songs written by Smashing Pumpkins' Billy Corgan and former Go-Go's guitarist Charlotte Caffey.

The Music: Hole's Breakthrough Single: "Miss World" (1994)

Did you know? *Rolling Stone* and the *Village Voice* rated Hole one of the top bands of 1995.

Courtney received a 1996 Golden Globe nomination for Best Actress for her role as Althea Flynt in *The People vs. Larry Flynt*.

She played a small role in the 1986 film *Sid and Nancy*, a screen depiction of the love affair between the Sex Pistols' Sid Vicious and Nancy Spungen, his American groupie girlfriend.

> **COURTNEY'S FILMS:**
> *Sid and Nancy, Love Kills, Straight to Hell, Feeling Minnesota, The People vs. Larry Flynt, 200 Cigarettes,* and *Man on the Moon*

Gary Lucas

Born: June 20, 1952

Talent: Guitarist/producer

The Road to Fame: Lucas has been playing guitar since he was nine years old and he hasn't put the instrument down too much since. He made a name for himself in the last incarnation of Captain Beefheart's Magic Band, for being able to tackle Beefheart's seemingly impossible compositions. Since the dissolution of the Magic Band, he has worked and recorded with such artists as Lou Reed, Nick Cave, Iggy Pop, Joan Osborne, Bryan Ferry, Jeff Buckley, the Future Sound of London, Patti Smith, Matthew Sweet, Adrian Sherwood, DJ Spooky, and many more. In addition to solo shows ranging from acoustic to electronic, Lucas has toured Europe accompanying the classic film *The Golem*. He also writes, records, and tours with his longtime power trio, Gods and Monsters.

The Music: Albums: *Gods and Monsters* (1992), *Evangeline* (1997), *Busy Being Born* (1998), *Improve the Shining Hour* (2000)

With Captain Beefheart: *Ice Cream for Crow* (1981)

Did you know? In 1973, Lucas played guitar for the European premiere of composer/conductor Leonard Bernstein's *Mass* in Vienna.

Lucas was once employed in the marketing department of Epic Records. His crowning achievement was coming up with the slogan "The Only Band That Matters" for the Clash.

He regularly contributes music for various ABC network documentary shows (*20/20*, *PrimeTime Live*).

Lucas cowrote and performed "Mojo Pin" with the late Jeff Buckley.

Barry Manilow

Born: Barry Alan Pincus, June 17, 1946—Brooklyn, NY

Talent: Singer/songwriter

The Road to Fame: After receiving a piano for his bar mitzvah, Barry began to gig at weddings and other functions playing jazz and Broadway show tunes. He continued to hone his vocal chops singing in the subway stations of Manhattan, and eventually enrolled at Julliard. At age eighteen he was hired to arrange music for TV and radio commercials. Years of additional training in piano bars led to his position as arranger for Bette Midler's first two albums and a subsequent album deal of his own. The success of his second record set the stage for his ensuing domination of the 1970s pop charts. An established pop icon by the 1980s, Manilow turned to recording jazz and pop standards. In the 1990s, he returned to his 1970s roots and continued to maintain his popularity as a live act.

The Music: Chart Toppers: "Mandy" (1972), "Could It Be Magic" (1972), "I Write the Songs" (1975), "Copacabana" (1978)

Assorted Work: *Barry Manilow* (1972), *Tryin' to Get the Feeling* (1975), *Live* (1977), *2:00 AM Paradise Café* (1984), *Swing Street* (1987), *Summer of '78* (1996), *Manilow Sings Sinatra* (1998)

Did you know? Barry took his mother's maiden name, Manilow, after his father abandoned the family.

Beginning in 1972, Manilow was Bette Midler's piano accompanist during her years as a performer in New York's gay bathhouses.

Before switching to music school, Barry had enrolled at City College as an advertising major.

> **BARRY TALKS:**
> "Every Jewish kid in my neighborhood had an accordion dumped in their laps as soon as they could lift the thing—they strapped it on me!"

Dick Manitoba

The Dictators

Born: Richard Blum, January 29, 1954

Talent: Lead singer

The Road to Fame: Dick was hired as the frontman of the Dictators not long after their formation in 1974. As one of the first New York punk bands, their groundbreaking songs—centering on pop culture, unrepentant rebellion, and personal excess—soon earned them major-label attention and industry buzz. But after the release of their 1975 Epic Records debut, *Go Girl Crazy!*, critics, radio, and their label reacted negatively, and the band never entered the mainstream. Despite the commercial backlash, the Dictators succeeded as heroes of the underground punk scene until their breakup in 1978. After reuniting briefly in 1981 for a live album, Dick formed the heavy Manitoba's Wild Kingdom, with former Dictators Andy Shernoff and Ross "The Boss" Funichello. In 1991, the Dictators reformed to embark on a much-lauded European tour.

The Music: The Dictators' Albums: *Go Girl Crazy!* (1975), *Manifest Destiny* (1977), *Bloodbrothers* (1978), *Live: Fuck 'Em if They Can't Take a Joke* (1981)

Did you know? Dick served as the Dictators' roadie shortly before becoming their lead singer.

His band nickname was "Handsome" Dick Manitoba.

He was once a professional wrestler.

Cheap Trick and AC/DC once opened for the Dictators.

Manfred Mann

Born: Manfred Lubowitz, October 21, 1940—Johannesburg, South Africa

Talent: Keyboardist/songwriter

The Road to Fame: Jazz keyboardist Mann hooked up with singer Paul Jones to form the R&B group Manfred Mann. After securing a significant following in Britain, the band moved towards a more pop-rock direction and scored hits in the United States with a couple of girl-group covers. Mike D'Abo replaced Jones after he departed in 1966 and helped maintain the band's popularity in Great Britain until its breakup in 1971. Manfred went on to form Manfred Mann's Earth Band, a straight-ahead rock group that recorded throughout the 1970s and early 1980s.

The Music: **Manfred Mann's Hit Singles**: "Do Wah Diddy Diddy," "Sha La La," "Come Tomorrow," "Pretty Flamingo," "The Mighty Quinn"

Earth Band's Hit Singles: "Blinded by the Light," "Spirit in the Night" (both written by Bruce Springsteen), "You Angel You" (written by Bob Dylan)

Did you know? One of the reasons Manfred Mann left his home country of South Africa in late 1961 was his growing disdain for South Africa's apartheid policies.

After moving to England, Mann kept money in his pocket by playing jazz, teaching music theory, and writing for *Jazz News* under the psuedonym "Manfred Manne." Eventually, he dropped the "e".

Manfred Mann scored hits with numerous other Bob Dylan penned tunes, including "With God on Our Side," "If You Gotta Go, Go Now" and "Just Like a Woman."

Barry Mann and Cynthia Weil

Born: Barry Mann: February 9, 1939—Brooklyn, NY
Cynthia Weil: October 18, 1937—New York, NY

Talent: Songwriters

The Road to Fame: Shortly after Barry dropped out of architecture school to become a full-time songwriter, he penned the hit single "She Say (Oom Dooby Doom)" for the Diamonds in 1959. He became a staff songwriter for Aldon Music at the Brill Building, where he met his soon-to-be wife/songwriter partner Cynthia Weil. Like Carole King and Gerry Goffin, the two became a hit songwriting powerhouse of the 1960s. In addition to their continuing collaboration in the ensuing decades as well as their establishment of Dyad Music Publishing, each pursued separate projects with other writers, recording artists, and film composers.

The Music: **The Mann and Weil Hit Machine:** "He's Sure the Boy I Love" (The Crystals), "Magic Town" (The Vogues), "Uptown" (The Crystals), "Blame It on the Bossa Nova" (Eydie Gorme), "(You're My) Soul and Inspiration" (The Righteous Brothers), "Here You Come Again" (Dolly Parton)

Did you know? Before trying her hand at songwriting, Cynthia originally trained as an actress and dancer.

In 1961, Barry recorded his only hit, "Who Put the Bomp (In the Bomp, Bomp, Bomp)," cowritten by Brill Building crony Gerry Goffin.

In addition to working with Lionel Richie, Cynthia cowrote "He's So Shy" (The Pointer Sisters) with Tom Snow.

The Righteous Brothers' biggest hit, "You've Lost That Lovin' Feelin' "—which Barry and Cynthia cowrote with Phil Spector—recently surpassed John Lennon and Paul McCartney's "Yesterday" as the most played song in history.

Malcolm McLaren

Born: January 22, 1946—London, England

Talent: Producer/manager/promoter/ recording artist/songwriter

The Road to Fame: After attending a variety of European art schools in the late 1960s, McLaren began designing clothing and opened up Sex, a London fashion boutique that catered to the punk crowd. It was out of Sex's regular clientele that he put together a house band known as the Sex Pistols. Having been the manager of the New York Dolls, Malcolm was already a savvy promoter, and he soon brought the Pistols into the limelight. After three astonishingly successful but turbulent years, the band fell apart and Malcolm's relationship with the surviving members (bassist Sid Vicious had killed himself) ended in discord. The early 1980s brought him renewed success, however, as he discovered and produced artists such as Adam Ant, Boy George, and Bow Wow Wow. In 1983, he began to record his own postmodern albums in which he blended rap, rock, funk, opera, and classical styles. While continuing his career as a recording artist, Malcolm also dabbled in film production and contemporary art.

The Music: Malcolm Sings . . . **Sort Of:** *Duck Rock* (1983), *Fans* (1984), *Waltz Darling* (1989), *Paris* (1994)

Memorable Tracks: "Buffalo Gals," "Soweto," "Duck for the Oyster," "Blue Danube," "Paris Paris"

Did you know? Malcolm headed CBS Theatrical Productions in 1985. Within a year of his arrival, the company folded.

Bootsy Collins and guitarist Jeff Beck lent Malcolm a hand on *Waltz Darling*, widely considered by critics and fans to be his finest album.

> **FILMS PRODUCED:**
> The Great Rock 'n' Roll Swindle (1980), The Ghosts of Oxford Street (1991)

Serch, bottom

MC Serch
3rd Bass

Born: Michael Berrin, May 6, 1967 —
Queens, NY

Talent: Rapper/songwriter

The Road to Fame: In 1987, Serch teamed up with Columbia University student and fellow white rapper Pete Nice (Peter J. Nash) and DJ Richie Rich, an African-American, to form the rap group 3rd Bass. The bi-racial group received not only commercial acclaim for their albums but the respect of the hardcore rap establishment as well. After 3rd Bass disbanded in 1992, Serch went solo and released *Return of the Product* later that same year.

The Music: Albums with 3rd Bass: *The Cactus Album* (1989), *Cactus Revisited* (1990), *Derelicts of Dialect* (1991)

Bass Hits: "The Gas Face," "Wordz of Wizdom," "Brooklyn Queens," "Pop Goes the Weasel"

Solo Shot: "Here It Comes"

Did you know? Serch, who grew up in Far Rockaway, Queens, attended the High School of Music and Art with Slick Rick and Dana Dane.

3rd Bass featured squinty-eyed, loud-mouthed comedian Gilbert Gottfried in all of their videos in some form.

MC Serch now runs his own consulting company, Serchlite, and helped get Nas his first major label deal.

MC SERCH ON RAPPIN' AND BEING JEWISH:

"I think that our suffering brings our communities together. Bottom line. I think the Jewish population and the black population has suffered the most carnage. We relate to pain. We relate to being ghetto-ized. Judaism is a respective religion, that's why most people think it's a nationality. African-American and African music is all cultural and I think that's the connection."

Do you think there's any chance of uniting the Jewish rappers of the world to form one collective entity? Maybe the Matzah Mobb or something?

"The Matzah Mobb? Wow! Somebody said something to me that we should form a crew and call it the Sons of David. No, that's not happenin'. Unless I see those cats in Temple, that's not happenin'. We'll call the group the Minion or the Ten Men. The Ten Men is hot. The Matzah Mafia, that's just crazy. That just sounds to me like the 2 Jive Jews type stuff. That's dead."

—Strength Magazine (www.strengthmag.com)

Mendel, left

Nate Mendel
Foo Fighters

Born: December 2, 1968—Seattle, WA

Talent: Bass guitarist

The Road to Fame: Mendel started his musical career in the late 1980s playing in various hardcore punk bands in the Pacific Northwest. He joined Sunny Day Real Estate, the celebrated "emo-core" band who struck a chord in the American underground rock scene and became notorious for refusing to do interviews. When SDRE disbanded in 1995, prior to the release of their untitled second album, Mendel and drummer William Goldsmith were asked to join Foo Fighters, the new band founded by former Nirvana drummer Dave Grohl. In 1997, SDRE regrouped and Goldsmith returned, but Mendel chose to remain with Foo Fighters.

The Music: With **Sunny Day Real Estate:** *Diary* (1994), *LP2* (aka *The Pink Album*, 1995)

With **Foo Fighters:** *The Colour and the Shape* (1997), *There Is Nothing Left to Lose* (1999)

Did you know? Mendel used to play in the provocative hardcore band Christ on a Crutch.

Early in 2000, Mendel stirred up the ire of AIDS activists by publicly supporting the teachings of the Alive and Well AIDS Alternatives group, an organization that claims HIV does not cause AIDS. Mendel told a reporter that Alive and Well "turned [the Foo Fighters] from an apolitical band to a political one."

Bette Midler

Born: December 1, 1945—Patterson, NJ

Talent: Singer/actress

The Road to Fame: Graduating from the University of Hawaii with a degree in drama, Bette moved to New York in 1965 and soon landed a role in the Broadway production of *Fiddler on the Roof*. Shortly thereafter, she began singing in gay bathhouses around the city. Her immense popularity there and on Broadway led to a record contract and her first release in 1972, for which she was awarded the Grammy for Best New Artist. After receiving a Tony later that year, Bette went on to record several platinum albums and make numerous TV appearances. Her movie career began with a 1979 Oscar-nominated role in *The Rose*. In the late 1980s she formed a film production company with Bonnie Bruckheimer, scoring big with the hit *Beaches*. Bette released *Some People's Lives*, which featured "From a Distance," a tribute to U.S. soldiers fighting in the Persian Gulf, in 1990, and went on to win Grammys, Emmys, and star in memorable films throughout the 1990s. Her concerts continue to sell out internationally.

The Music: Debut Album: *The Divine Miss M* (1972)

Latest Release: *Bathhouse Betty* (1998), featuring songs recorded by Van Halen's first producer, Ted Templeman.

Did you know? Bette's parents named her after Bette Davis, but mispronounced her name as "bet."

Bette officially entered show business as an extra in George Roy Hill's *Hawaii*.

Barry Manilow was Bette's musical director in the days when she performed in the New York bathhouses.

Bette's makeup artist gave her the name "Miss M."

> **OTHER FILM ROLES:**
> *Down and Out in Beverly Hills, Ruthless People, Outrageous Fortune, Big Business, Get Shorty, The First Wives Club*

Keith Morris

The Circle Jerks

Talent: Singer/songwriter

Morris, second from right

The Road to Fame: Beginning in 1977, Keith sang lead vocals for the groundbreaking hardcore band Black Flag before departing two years later to form the Circle Jerks with guitarist Greg Hetson. With a constantly changing rhythm section, the band sporadically recorded a series of cult albums through the 1980s and 1990s, fueled by Keith's satirical lyrics and Greg's biting guitar riffs.

The Music: With Black Flag: *Nervous Breakdown* (1978)

More Jerk Classics: "Wasted," "Beverly Hills," "Letter Bomb," "Killing for Jesus," "Wild in the Streets," "When the Shit Hits the Fan"

Did you know? While growing up in Manhattan Beach, Keith heard the Doors practicing in a garage adjacent to a friend's house.

Keith had to convince Debbie Gibson's mom that the subject of the song Debbie would later sing with the Circle Jerks, "I Wanna Destroy You," was television violence.

In 2000, maverick punk label Epitaph released the debut record from Keith's new band, Midget Handjob.

> **THE EARLY INFLUENCES:**
> The Who, the Kinks, the Rolling Stones, the Animals, the Doors, the Standells, the Seeds

Randy Newman

Born: November 28, 1943 — New Orleans, LA

Talent: Singer/songwriter/film composer

The Road to Fame: Shortly after dropping out of UCLA, Randy began as a career singer-songwriter with a poppy R&B sensibility and a penchant for satirical lyrics. His initial recorded material had little commercial impact, but his songwriting skills were quickly lauded, leading to writing gigs with many popular musicians. As a solo performer, Randy acquired a strong cult following in the 1970s. His biting wit on the 1978 single "Short People" led to protests and criticism, but the controversy made it a surprise hit. Ultimately, it was his career as a film composer — beginning in 1979 — that earned Newman worldwide acclaim.

The Music: Other Sardonic Singles: "Rednecks," "I Love L.A.," "It's Money That Matters"

Randy's Film Scores/Soundtracks: *Ragtime* (1981), *The Natural* (1984), *Down and Out in Beverly Hills* (1986), *Three Amigos!* (1987), *Parenthood* (1989), *Major League* (1989), *Blaze* (1990), *Avalon* (1990), *Awakenings* (1990), *The Paper* (1994), *Maverick* (1994), *Forrest Gump* (1994), *Toy Story* (1995), *James and the Giant Peach* (1996), *Michael* (1996)

Did you know? Randy wrote songs in the early 1970s for Judy Collins, Dusty Springfield, Peggy Lee, and Three Dog Night, who scored a number-one hit with his "Mama Told Me Not to Come."

Randy is the nephew of Alfred Newman, composer of the Twentieth Century Fox theme.

He has received eight Academy Award nominations for his film scores.

Director Wolfgang Petersen rejected his score for 1997's *Air Force One.*

In 1999, he recorded a pop album for DreamWorks, *Bad Love,* that was produced by noted alt-rock producer Mitchell Froom (Los Lobos, Latin Playboys, Suzanne Vega, Sheryl Crow).

Laura Nyro

Born: Laura Nigro, October 18, 1947—the Bronx, New York City

Died: April 9, 1997—Danbury, Connecticut

Talent: Singer/songwriter/pianist

The Road to Fame: The daughter of a jazz trumpeter, Nyro was hooked on music early in her life. Her idiosyncratic style was based upon a love for 1960s girl groups and pop songs, and much later, a respect for Bob Dylan and jazz progenitor John Coltrane. Drawing from these influences, Nyro made a name for herself as a gifted songwriter and a remarkable vocalist with interesting phrasing and a knack for dramatic intonation. Nyro was such a sensitive individual that acclaimed American critic Robert Christgau once wrote that Nyro "was born 150 years too late." Indeed, she retired from music and performing twice in her career (the first time at age 24). The intensely personal Nyro released one album in the 1980s (1985's *Mother's Spiritual*) and only two releases in the last decade. Sadly, several weeks after the release of the career-spanning anthology *Stoned Soul Picnic*, Nyro succumbed to ovarian cancer.

The Music: Suggested Listening: *Eli and the Thirteenth Confession* (1968), *Gonna Take a Miracle* (1971), *Walk the Dog and Light the Light* (1993), *Stoned Soul Picnic: The Best of Laura Nyro* (1997)

Did you know? Nyro was a prolific songwriter who wrote major hits for many bands in the 1960s and 1970s. Some of the enduring radio hits she penned include "Stoney End" (the title song of Barbra Streisand's 1970 album), "And When I Die" (recorded by Blood, Sweat & Tears in 1969, and written when Nyro was in her teens), "Eli's Comin'" (recorded by Three Dog Night the same year), and a string of hits for the popular soul/pop group the Fifth Dimension, including "Stoned Soul Picnic" (1968), "Wedding Bell Blues" (1969), and "Save the Country" (1970).

Her 1971 release, the rhythm-and-blues based *Gonna Take a Miracle*, was overseen by producers Kenny Gamble and Leon Huff and featured the participation of 1970s soul diva Labelle and the Sigma Sound studio band.

On the 1989 album, *Laura—Live at the Bottom Line*, Nyro's backing band was led by Jimmy Vivino, who currently appears as the guitarist in drummer Max Weinberg's house band on the NBC show *Late Night with Conan O'Brien*.

Phil Ochs

Born: December 19, 1940—El Paso, TX

Died: April 9, 1976—Far Rockaway, NY

Talent: Singer/songwriter

The Road to Fame: Phil found a welcome audience in young Americans with his civil rights– and anti-war–themed songs as he rose to the top of the folk pantheon in the early 1960s. In 1967, he ended his acoustic career, and like Dylan, he set off on an electric rock exploration. When his voice was permanently damaged after a 1970 mugging in Africa, Phil's career fell apart, which led to alcohol abuse and psychological problems. He took his own life in 1976.

The Music: **Memorable Songs**: "Power and the Glory," "Bound for Glory," "Draft Dodger Rag," "Love Me, I'm a Liberal," "Changes," "I Ain't Marching Anymore"

Did you know? Phil was friends with fellow folk icon Bob Dylan, who said of him: "I just can't keep up with Phil. And he's getting better and better and better."

He rallied with war protesters at the disastrous 1968 Democratic Convention in Chicago.

Perkins, top right

Stephen Perkins

Jane's Addiction and Porno for Pyros

Born: Stephen Andrew Perkins, September 13, 1967—Los Angeles, CA

Talent: Drummer/percussionist

The Road to Fame: In 1985, Steve was dating the sister of Jane's Addiction bassist Eric Avery, who invited him to join the band. When the band broke up in 1991, he went on to form Porno for Pyros with Jane's lead singer Perry Farrell. Even as a full-time drummer for the band, Steve has found time to lend his rhythmic expertise to other high-profile artists.

The Music: Collaborations: Nine Inch Nails, Ugly Kid Joe, No Doubt, Rage Against the Machine, and Infectious Grooves

Did you know? Steve was a childhood friend of Jane's guitarist Dave Navarro.

Steve and Dave Navarro joined their high-school marching band in Sherman Oaks, California—Steve went on to drum for the famed USC Trojans Marching Band.

Steve performed with Infectious Grooves in the film *Encino Man*.

He played a bongo solo in the film *Exit to Eden*.

On the Jane's Addiction home video *Soul Kiss*, Steve plays an entire percussion solo with spoons on bottles, pots, and pans.

He used his bar mitzvah money to buy his first drum kit.

In 1997, Steve formed a band called Banyan with Mike Watt (Minutemen/fIREHOSE), Nels Cline (the Geraldine Fibbers), and "Money Mark" Nishita (Beastie Boys keyboardist) that has since released two albums of experimental jazz-rock fusion.

Phranc

Born: Susan Gottlieb, 1958—Los Angeles, CA

Talent: Singer/songwriter

The Road to Fame: After years of performing with various punk bands, Phranc emerged as a modern folk solo artist in 1985 with her indie release *Folksinger*, an album that unabashedly trumpeted her own lesbianism. Critical praise led to her signing with Island, on which she released *I Enjoy Being a Girl* (1989), *Positively Phranc* (1991), and the 1995 EP *Goofyfoot*.

The Music: *Folksinger* (1985), *I Enjoy Being a Girl* (1989), *Positively Phranc* (1991), *Goofyfoot* (EP—1995), *Milkman* (1998)

Did you know? Phranc appeared in the punk-music documentary *The Decline of Western Civilization* (1981) as the bassist for art-punks Catholic Discipline.

Her song "Martina" is a tribute to tennis legend Martina Navratilova.

Phranc has performed in drag as Neil Diamond.

She has toured with some of the biggest names in 1980s "alternative" rock: the Violent Femmes, the Smiths, the Dead Kennedys, X, Hüsker Dü, and the Pogues.

In spring 2000, Phranc appeared on Donny and Marie Osmond's daytime talk show as one of the country's most successful Tupperware saleswomen. She even sang a song about it.

> **PHRANC-LY SPEAKING:**
> "I'm just your typical Jewish-American lesbian folksinger."

Monique Powell

Save Ferris

Born: August 20, 1975

Talent: Vocalist

Powell, center

The Road to Fame: The daughter of a Southern Baptist father and a Moroccan Jewish mother (her father converted), Powell started singing in various indie-pop bands before joining Orange County ska-pop hopefuls Save Ferris. The band financed their 1996 debut, *Introducing Save Ferris*, releasing it on their own Starpool imprint. When influential radio station KROQ put it in regular rotation, the demand for the record outweighed the band's financial ability to keep repressing the disc. The band soon signed with Epic, who rereleased the record with additional songs under the title *It Means Everything*.

The Music: Albums: *Save Ferris* (1997), *It Means Everything* (1997), *Modified* (1999)

Did you know? Save Ferris took their name from the Matthew Broderick movie *Ferris Bueller's Day Off*.

Before joining Save Ferris, Powell was a member of an experimental band called Larry, whose main influence was Frank Zappa.

When the L.A.-based radio station KROQ was compiling one of its annual Christmas charity compact discs, Powell rewrote the lyrics to the Waitresses' holiday song "Christmas Wrapping" and turned it into a Hanukah song. "To my knowledge nobody had ever done a popular Hanukah song other than Adam Sandler. And of course, I always wanted to be Adam Sandler!"

> **A QUOTABLE QUOTE:**
> "I was raised in Orange County and there's no Jews there," says Powell. "Not in Garden Grove, at least . . ."

Joey Ramone

The Ramones

Born: Jeffrey Hyman, May 19, 1952 —
Forest Hills, NY

Talent: Singer/songwriter

The Road to Fame: In 1974, Hyman became "Joey Ramone," drummer of the Ramones, a new punk-rock band whose members assumed the surname "Ramone," and dressed in leather and torn blue jeans. Joey switched to lead vocals shortly after the band began gigging in clubs with their trademark twenty-minute sets of two-minute songs. The Ramones' 1976 debut album quickly earned them cult status in the United States and Britain. Despite a few attempts to crossover into the pop charts in the early 1980s the Ramones maintained a consistent sound during their twenty-two-year existence. The 1996 Lollapalooza festival marked their last tour, after which Joey started a radio show, produced several bands, and began work on a collaborative recording project with singer Ronnie Spector of Ronettes fame for the indie-punk label Kill Rock Stars.

The Music: Suggested Listening: *Ramones* (1976), *The Ramones Leave Home* (1977), *Road to Ruin* (1978), *End of the Century* (1980), *Loco Live* (1991), *Acid Eaters* (1993)

Did you know? The Ramones recorded their debut album for only $6000.

Joey and the band played major roles in Roger Corman's *Rock 'n' Roll High School* (1979).

Road to Ruin was the first Ramones album to run over half an hour.

The legendary Phil Spector produced the Ramones' 1980 album, *End of the Century*.

In 1989, the Ramones wrote the theme song to the film adaptation of Stephen King's *Pet Sematary*.

The Ramones' appearance at the 1996 Lollapalooza was their farewell tour.

Lou Reed

Born: March 2, 1942—Freeport, NY

Talent: Singer/songwriter

The Road to Fame: Growing up as a fan of rock and R&B, Reed continued the rebellious, often somber poetry he began as a teen throughout college. Upon graduating, he worked as a songwriter for a small music publisher in New York City. It was there that he met bassist and Welsh classical musician John Cale. In 1965, the two formed the Velvet Underground with guitarist Sterling Morrison and drummer Angus Maclise. Maclise departed and was replaced by Maureen "Moe" Tucker. Pop-art icon Andy Warhol discovered them in Greenwich Village, and soon the band gained public notoriety and a recording contract, creating four highly influential studio albums that tackled issues such as drugs, suicide, sex, and depression. When the band broke up in 1970, Lou launched a solo career that—like the Velvets—produced few hits, but he was continually acclaimed for his pensive lyricism, as well as being credited with leading the way for other avant-garde rockers, including David Bowie. In 1993, the Velvets reunited for a brief tour.

The Music: **Assorted Velvet LPs:** *The Velvet Underground and Nico* (1967), *White Light/White Heat* (1967), *The Velvet Underground* (1969), *Loaded* (1970)

Velvet Classics: "Sweet Jane," "Heroin," "Sister Ray," "Rock and Roll," "Venus in Furs"

Assorted Solo Albums: *Transformer* (1972), *Sally Can't Dance* (1974), *Metal Machine Music* (1975), *Street Hassle* (1978), *The Blue Mask* (1982), *Magic and Loss* (1992), *Set the Twilight Reeling* (1996)

Classic Singles: "Wild Child," "Walk on the Wild Side," "I Wanna Be Black," "Dirt," "Vicious"

Did you know? As a teen, the rebellious Lou was treated with electroshock therapy.

He originally met Sterling Morrison in college at Syracuse University.

Hailed as one of the most important bands of all time, the Velvet Underground was inducted into the Rock and Roll Hall of Fame in 1996.

Jonathan Richman

Born: May 15, 1951 — Boston, MA

Talent: Singer/songwriter/guitarist

The Road to Fame: After only three years of guitar playing, Jonathan moved to New York in 1969, where he hung out with Warhol protégés the Velvet Underground and took on an assortment of odd jobs. When his decidedly eccentric music failed to attract a following, he headed back to Boston and formed the punkish pop band the Modern Lovers. The group broke up in 1973, three years before their self-titled debut album was released. Jonathan created a new acoustic/doo-wop version of Modern Lovers and released two albums in 1977. After releasing a string of cult-hit solo records from 1979 to 1985, he returned with Modern Lovers in 1986 and again went solo in 1990. His eclectic brand of pop stylings never made it into the mainstream, but he received ample national exposure from his appearance in the hit 1998 gross-out comedy, *There's Something About Mary.*

The Music: **Cult Classics**: "Roadrunner," "Ice Cream Man," "Pablo Picasso," "I'm a Little Aeroplane," "Hospital," "Egyptian Reggae"

Assorted Albums: *Jonathan Richman and the Modern Lovers* (1977), *Back in Your Life* (1979), *Jonathan Sings!* (1983), *Modern Lovers '88* (1988), *Jonathan Goes Country* (1990)

Did you know? Jonathan spent his first two weeks in New York in 1969, sleeping on the couch of the Velvet Underground's manager.

Jonathan sang his 1994 release, *Jonathan, Te Vas a Emocionar!*, entirely in Spanish.

Robbie Robertson

The Band

Born: Jaimie Robbie Robertson, July 5, 1943—Toronto, Ontario, Canada

Talent: Singer/songwriter/guitarist/producer

The Road to Fame: Robertson achieved fame as the principal songwriter for the Band, a group of Canadians that got together in the late fifties to back up rockabilly singer Ronnie Hawkins. After finishing their stint with Hawkins, the group played club gigs and wrote their own music steeped in deep Americana. They soon came to the attention of Bob Dylan, who hired them as a backup group for his historic "electric" 1965–66 world tour. After the tour, the band settled in a farmhouse in upstate New York to record their debut album for Capitol. That album, *Music from Big Pink*, featured such Robertson-penned radio classics as "This Wheel's on Fire" and "The Weight" and established them on American FM radio. The Band continued throughout the 1970s with a string of critically and commercially well-received albums entrenched in country, blues, and honky-tonk idioms. Upon the completion of their 1975 album *Northern Lights, Southern Cross*, the members felt the group had run its course, so the band recorded a live album, *The Last Waltz*, which was recorded Thanksgiving Day 1976 at the Winterland Auditorium in San Francisco. A documentary of the event was filmed by acclaimed director Martin Scorsese for theatrical release. In the early- and mid-1980s, the Band did several reunion tours, but Robertson refused to participate.

The Music: Suggested Listening: With the Band: *Music from Big Pink* (1968), *Stage Fright* (1970), *Rock of Ages* (1972)

With Bob Dylan: *The Basement Tapes* (1975), *Blood on the Tracks* (1975)

Solo: *Robbie Robertson* (1987)

Did you know? Robertson produced Neil Diamond's 1976 album, *Beautiful Noise*.

Robertson appeared in the 1980 Scorsese film *Carny*, and has supplied the scores for some of the director's other films.

His self-titled 1987 solo album featured "Fallen Angel," a tribute to Band keyboardist Richard Manuel, who had committed suicide after a Band reunion gig in Florida in 1986.

Robertson immersed himself in the world of trip-hop by working with acclaimed producer Howie B (U2, Bjork, Skylab) on the 1998 release, *Contact from the Underworld of Redboy*.

David Lee Roth

Born: October 10, 1955—Bloomington, IN.

Talent: Singer/songwriter/band-leader

The Road to Fame: The son of an ophthalmologist, Dave channeled his childhood hyperactivity into making music, becoming the charismatic lead vocalist for the Pasadena-based rock group Red Ball Jets in the early 1970s. After renting his PA system out to the Van Halen bothers, guitarist Eddie and drummer Alex, Dave saw their group Mammoth and was dazzled. Equally impressed by Dave's wild showmanship and raw vocal energy, the brothers hired him as their lead singer, adding bassist Michael Anthony soon after. Mammoth became Van Halen and soon became the hottest rock band in the L.A. area. In 1977, Dave and the boys were signed with Warner Brothers, after which they went on to release *Van Halen* and five subsequent multi-platinum albums, becoming the most popular and influential hard-rock band of the late 1970s and early 1980s. Their reputation for wild partying and juvenile antics—much of which was attributed to"Diamond Dave"—earned them the title "The Ultimate Party Band." After touring behind their most popular record, *1984*, Dave split from Van Halen acrimoniously and embarked on a successful solo career beginning with his EP *Crazy from the Heat* and debut LP *Eat 'Em and Smile*. He reunited briefly with Van Halen in 1996 to record two new tracks for a "best-of" Van Halen collection.

Dave on Being a Rock Star: "It's excessive. In terms of the fringe benefits you're supposed to get from rock and roll, I'd say we're black belts."

The Music: Hits with Van Halen: "You Really Got Me," "Jamie's Cryin'," "Dance the Night Away," "Everybody Wants Some," "Unchained," "Oh, Pretty Woman," "Jump," "Panama," "Hot for Teacher"

Solo Hits: "California Girls," "Just a Gigolo," "Yankee Rose," "Going Crazy," "Just Like Paradise," "Stand Up," "A Little Ain't Enough"

Did you know? Dave played Vegas at the MGM Grand in 1996.

KISS bassist Gene Simmons "discovered" Van Halen, producing their first demo and helping them to get signed with Warner Brothers.

Dave began listening to his idol and fellow-Jew Al Jolson at age seven.

He's a black belt in karate.

Dave's autobiography, *Crazy from the Heat,* was published in 1997.

Adam Sandler

Born: September 9, 1966—Brooklyn, N.Y.

Talent: Comedian/singer-songwriter

The Road to Fame: Raised in Manchester, N. H., Adam's first real brush with comedy came at age seventeen when his brother told him that he should take the stage at a Boston comedy club. While studying at N.Y.U., Adam honed his comedy chops in clubs and at college campuses around the city. Shortly after graduation in 1990, he was hired as a writer/cast member of *Saturday Night Live*, becoming one of the show's most popular performers. In 1995, two years after the release of his Grammy-nominated comedy album *They're All Gonna Laugh at You!*, which contained the hit single "Lunchlady Land," Adam left *SNL* to pursue a career in both stand-up comedy and movies.

The Music: Sandler's Other Hit Singles: "The Thanksgiving Song," "The Chanukah Song," "What the Hell Happened to Me?"

Follow-Up Albums: *What the Hell Happened to Me?* (1996), *What's Your Name* (1997), *Stan & Judy's kid* (1999)

> **FILMS STARRING ADAM SANDLER:**
> *Billy Madison* (1995), *Happy Gilmore* (1996), *The Wedding Singer* (1998), *The Waterboy* (1998), *Big Daddy* (1999), *Little Nicky* (2000).

Did you know? Adam's first professional gig involved a comedic appearance on "Showtime at the Apollo."

His 1996 comedy album *What the Hell Happened to Me?* reached the Top 20 and went double platinum.

Adam wrote the screenplays for *Billy Madison, Happy Gilmore, The Waterboy, Big Daddy,* and *Little Nicky* with his college roommate Tim Herlihy (not a Jew).

Neil Sedaka

Born: March 13, 1939—Brooklyn, NY

Talent: Songwriter/singer/pianist

The Road to Fame: While training at Juilliard, Neil scored his first songwriting hit in 1958 with "Stupid Cupid." A subsequent recording contract with RCA landed him in the Brill Building, where he worked alongside other notable Tin Pan Alley singer/songwriters including Carol King and Gerry Goffin. Neil recorded his own hits from the late 1950s through the early 1960s but shifted his focus to writing for other artists at the end of that decade. He reinvented himself as a pop singer in the 1970s and became widely popular in England. Though his career as a recording artist essentially ended in the 1980s, he continues successful perennial touring as a live performer.

The Music: Pop Hits: "Oh Carol," "The Diary," "Stairway to Heaven," "Calendar Girl," "Next Door to an Angel," "Happy Birthday, Sweet Sixteen," "Breaking Up Is Hard to Do"

Did you know? Neil recorded on Elton John's Rocket label in the mid 1970s.

His hit "Oh Carol" was a tribute to friend Carole King.

Silver, second from left

Josh Silver
Type O Negative

Born: November 14, 1962 —
Brooklyn, NY

Talent: Keyboardist/arranger/
producer

The Road to Fame: Silver started playing piano at eight years old and had been in a series of different cover bands through his teens and early twenties. In the mid-eighties he joined a Brooklyn-based hair-metal band, Original Sin, and soon started his collection of body piercings and tattoos. In 1989, old friend Pete Steele offered Silver an invite to join his new band, Type O Negative, which has been described as "gothadelic industrimental."

Albums: *Slow, Deep and Hard* (1991), *Bloody Kisses* (1993), *World Coming Down* (1999)

Did you know? When asked about his past accomplishments, the brutally honest Silver laughed and said that he was "no big deal."

A SLICE OF LIFE ANECDOTE:
"I was rejected by eighty percent of my very Jewish neighborhood, Orthodox and Hassidim. About two years ago, I had a religious man come to my home—payes, coat, hat—full gear. He was looking for mezuzahs on the door, which I have. Now there's no air conditioning in my house, so I'm shirtless. I opened the door and he says, 'I'm sorry, I thought a Jew lived here.' When I insisted I was a Jew, he backed away from the door and almost fell down my steps. This is probably going to be very unpopular in your book, I'm sorry to say."

oomfield MarcBolan MICHAELBoltonIgorCavaleraLEONARD COF
an dannyelfman DONALDFAGEN PerryFarrellNickFeldman DougFeig
rtGarfunkel AdamGaynor GerryGoffin NINAGORDO
SusannaHoffs ScottIan BillyJOEL MickJONES Ira Kapla
nyKRAVITZ GettyLee JerryLeiber & MikeStoller KEITHLevi
rry Manilow DickManitoba BarryMANN Cynthia WE
dler KeithMORRIS Randy Newman NOFX LauraNYRO HILOc
hanRichman DavidLeeRoth ADAMSANDLER NeilSEDAKAJosh Silv
illSobule PhilSpector Paul Stanley ChrisSTEINSteveSt

Simmons, bottom right

Gene Simmons

KISS

Born: Chaim Whitz, August 25, 1949—Haifa, Israel

Talent: Bassist/songwriter/actor

The Road to Fame: Becoming "Gene Klein" and later "Gene Simmons" after arriving in America as a child, Gene took up bass at age sixteen, but only committed to a career in rock music after a brief stint as a sixth-grade teacher upon finishing college. After working his way through a series of bands, he finally landed in Wicked Lester in 1972 with singer/guitarist Paul Stanley. The two left the band to form their own group, recruiting drummer Peter Criscoula (Peter Criss) and lead guitarist Paul Frehley (Ace Frehley) to form KISS in 1973. A small-label record deal brought forth their self-titled debut album the following year. By 1977 they'd become the most popular band in America, known not only for their heavy sound but their trademark makeup and stage pyrotechnics. Gene's fire-breathing and blood-spitting stage antics set the standard for heavy metal showmanship. After Criss and Frehley left the band in the early 1980s, Gene and Paul Stanley hired replacements and retired the makeup for *Lick It Up*. Gene also pursued several film acting roles at this time. Despite the waning popularity of the band, they continued to produce platinum albums through the 1990s. The original band members were reunited for a live album and tour that proved to be the most successful in the industry for 1996.

Hits: "Deuce" (1974), "Strutter" (1974), "Detroit Rock City" (1977), "Lick It Up" (1983), "Rock 'n' Roll All Nite" (1988), "Forever" (1989)

Gene on Religion: "The beautiful idea of religion, that the meek shall inherit the earth, is naivete at its highest. The strong inherit the earth; the meek inherit shit."

—*Bass Player*, 1996

Movies: *Kiss Meets the Phantom of the Park* (1978), *Runaway* (1984), *Trick or Treat* (1986), *The Decline of Western Civilization Part 2* (1988), *Wanted: Dead or Alive* (1987), *Red* (1990), *Surf* (1990)

Did you know? As a teen, Gene worked as an assistant to editors at *Vogue* and *Glamour* magazines.

Gene ran a typing service in college—he could type ninety words per minute.

He speaks fluent Hebrew, Hungarian, German, and Japanese.

Gene does not drink, smoke, or do drugs, and he has no tattoos.

He once managed singer/actress Liza Minelli.

His tongue is *seven* inches long.

Carly Simon

Born: June 25, 1945—New York City, New York

Talent: Singer/songwriter/keyboardist/author

The Road to Fame: The daughter of the co-founder of the publishing company Simon & Schuster, Simon dropped out of college to play in the Simon Sisters, a folk-based duo with her sister, Lucy. When her sister got married, Carly continued as a solo act, but became disheartened after sessions for her debut record (featuring Al Koooper, Michael Bloomfield, and members of the Band) were abandoned. She returned to music in 1970, when Elektra Records founder Jac Holzman signed her to his label as a solo artist, reportedly against the wishes of his staff. Simon scored a Top 10 hit immediately ("That's The Way I Always Heard It Should Be" from her self-titled debut), which was the first of a string of major hits (including "Anticipation," "You're So Vain," and "Haven't Got Time for the Pain") she had throughout the 1970s and 1980s.

The Music: Suggested Listening: *Anticipation* (1971), *No Secrets* (1972), *Boys in the Trees* (1978), *Torch* (1981), *Letters Never Sent* (1994), *The Bedroom Tapes* (2000)

Did you know? Simon married singer/songwriter James Taylor in 1972. They have two children, and divorced in 1983.

Simon has had numerous successes supplying songs for such films as *Postcards from the Edge* ("You Are the Love of My Life"), *Working Girl* ("Let the River Run"), *Heartburn* ("Coming Around Again"), and *The Spy Who Loved Me* ("Nobody Does It Better").

The late Jackie Onassis approached the singer to write her memoirs for a book. Simon was uncomfortable with the idea, and instead wrote her first children's book, *Amy, the Dancing Bear*, which was published in 1988. Since then, Simon has penned three additional children's books.

In 1975, Simon lived in a house on Rockingham Drive in Los Angeles. Nearly two decades later, the house became notorious as the home where O. J. Simpson was living at the time of his wife's murder.

Paul Simon

Born: October 13, 1941—Newark, NJ

Talent: Singer/songwriter

The Road to Fame: Paul's professional career officially began at sixteen with his hit "Hey Schoolgirl," recorded with school chum Art Garfunkel. While Art went off to college, Paul continued to pursue music, recording with the group Tico and the Triumphs and going solo as "Jerry Landis." In 1964, he reteamed with Garfunkel and released *Wednesday Morning 3 A.M.* on Columbia. It took a year for the album to hit and, as a result of a remixed rock version of "The Sound of Silence," Simon and Garfunkel became household names. After many successful LPs, singles, and tours, the duo released their most popular album, *Bridge over Troubled Water* in 1970, but broke up shortly thereafter. Paul immediately went to work as a solo artist and achieved enormous success starting with a self-titled LP in 1972. His biggest-selling release came over a decade later with his South African music–inspired *Graceland* (1986). Aside from the occasional reunions with Art Garfunkel, Paul has since maintained his status as one of America's favorite singer/songwriters through continued hit solo releases and tours.

The Music: Solo Hits: "Mother and Child Reunion" (1972), "50 Ways to Leave Your Lover" (1975), "Late in the Evening" (1972), "Loves Me Like a Rock" (1973)

Other Big Solo Albums: *There Goes Rhymin' Simon* (1973), *Still Crazy After All These Years* (1975), *Hearts and Bones* (1983), *The Rhythm of the Saints* (1990)

Did you know? Paul starred in and wrote the soundtrack for the Warner Brothers film *One Trick Pony* (1980).

He has won two Grammy Awards for Album of the Year: *Still Crazy After All These Years* (1975) and *Graceland* (1986).

Slash

Guns N' Roses

Born: Saul Hudson, July 23, 1965 —
Stroke-on-Trent, Staffordshire, England

Talent: Songwriter/guitarist

The Road to Fame: The son of an interracial couple, Slash grew up in Los Angeles, where he taught himself guitar as a teenager. He soon began jamming with drummer Steven Adler and later added bassist Duff McKagan to form Road Crew. Finally, in 1985, Slash and his friends joined Axl Rose and Izzy Stradlin, whose band Guns N' Roses had just lost guitarist Traci Guns. Guns N' Roses' 1987 full-length debut for Geffen, *Appetite for Destruction*, proved to be a phenomenal breakthrough for the band, earning them fame, perpetual airplay, and world tours, during which Slash became famous for his nonstop boozing. After the release of their successful acoustic EP, *Lies*, Stradlin departed and Adler was fired for drug dependency. Despite a three-year hiatus, their two-volume release *Use Your Illusion I* and *II* dominated the charts in 1991. The release of their punk-tinged covers record, *The Spaghetti Incident*, marked Slash's departure. While singer Axl Rose wanted to pursue a more industrial-rock sound, Slash remained a devotee of blues-based rock, putting together a new band, Slash's Snakepit.

The Music: G N' R Hits: "Welcome to the Jungle" (1987), "Sweet Child o' Mine" (1987), "Paradise City" (1987), "Mr. Brownstone" (1987), "Patience" (1989), "One in a Million" (1989), "November Rain" (1991), "Yesterday" (1991), "You Could Be Mine" (1991)

Did you know? Slash got his nickname from the druggy father of a neighborhood friend in Los Angeles.

When growing up in Los Angeles, his African-American mother (a clothing designer) and his English Jewish father (an art director for record covers) played host at their L.A. house to such music celebrities as Neil Young, Joni Mitchell, David Bowie, Ron Wood, Iggy Pop, and David Geffen.

Slash's first guitar was a one-string acoustic that he found in his grandmother's house.

He has recorded or performed with Michael Jackson, Jeff Beck, Iggy Pop, Alice Cooper, Eric Clapton, Lenny Kravitz, Paul Rogers, Joe Perry, and Brian May.

The U.S. Surgeon General nixed a deal Slash had prepared to make with Black Death Vodka in 1992, claiming it would have had a bad influence on the youth of America.

Hillel Slovak

The Red Hot Chili Peppers

Died: July 27, 1988—Los Angeles, CA

Talent: Guitarist

The Road to Fame: Hillel befriended drummer Jack Irons as an L.A. teen and formed the band Anthem. Soon the duo joined singer Alain Johannes and formed the band What Is This. During this time, Hillel and Jack did some one-off shows with their longtime friends Michael "Flea" Balzary and Anthony Kiedis's new band, the Red Hot Chili Peppers. After one EP and a few songs on What Is This's MCA debut, Hillel rejoined his buddies in the Peppers to record their second album, *Freaky Styley* (1985). In 1987, Irons rejoined the fold, and the original band of merry men recorded the third Peppers album, *The Uplift Mofo Party Plan*. Shortly after the album's release and on the verge of international success, Hillel died of a heroin overdose.

The Music: Albums with the Band: *The Red Hot Chili Peppers* (1984), *Freaky Styley* (1985), *The Uplift Mofo Party Plan* (1987)

Flea on Hillel: "Hillel changed my life. If it wasn't for Hillel, there's no way I'd be sitting here now, because he turned me onto rock music."

George Clinton on Hillel: "Hillel knew exactly what he wanted. His first run of a solo would always be really slick and jazzy and articulated, just to impress you, and then he'd play it real fast with a punk edge."

Main Influences: Jimi Hendrix and KISS

Did you know? In 1999, Hillel's brother James compiled a book, *Behind the Sun*, that featured photos of Hillel's artwork, personal diary entries, and unpublished photographs.

Dee Snider
Twisted Sister

Born: March 15, 1955—Long Island, NY

Talent: Singer/actor/screenwriter/disc jockey

The Road to Fame: As the frontman for heavy metal heroes Twisted Sister, Snider used crossdressing, makeup, and sexually charged lyrics as hooks to rise above the NYC bar-band competition. After every major label in America passed on signing the band, Snider and his bandmates secured a record deal in 1982 from the British label Secret, who released TS's debut, *Under the Blade*. In America, the Atlantic label wised up, signed the band, and in 1984 released *Stay Hungry*, which spawned the hit teen-rebel anthem "We're Not Gonna Take It." The following year, Twisted Sister followed up the multiplatinum *Hungry* with *Come Out and Play*, an album which paled in comparison to their previous success. Infighting within the ranks of the Sisterhood broke the band up in 1987, and Snider carried the rock torch in a series of post-TS bands as SMF and Widowmaker.

The Music: Suggested Listening: *Stay Hungry* (1984)

Did you know? In 1984, when the Parents' Music Resource Center demanded a Congressional inquiry into the content of popular music lyrics, Snider testified in front of a Congressional committee along with Frank Zappa and John Denver.

In 1999, Snider wrote the screenplay and played the role of a sex-crazed psychopath on the Internet in the horror film *Strangeland*.

In 2000, Snider landed a job as a radio personality in Long Island, NY. His '80s metal show, *The House of Hair*, is syndicated to a vast network of radio stations throughout America.

bAlpertJudahBauerBeastieBoys Beck RayBenson ERICBLOOM
mmyDavisJr. NEIL DIAMOND AdamDurwitz Bob Dylan Jan
sohFinn AlanFreed MartyFriedman JUSTINEFRISCHMANN Ker
terGreen BrettGurewitz RICHARDHELL GregHetson Peter Hir
veKatz LenNYKaye CaroleKing MarkKnopfler ALKoop
Loeb CourtneyLove GARY LUCAS Mamas and the Papa
nfredMann Malcolm McClaren MC SEARCH NateMendel Ber
phenPerkins MoniquePowell Phranc JoeyRamone LouReed

Jill Sobule

Born: January 16, 1961 — Denver, CO

Talent: Singer/songwriter/instrumentalist

The Road to Fame: Jill began her professional career during a college vacation in Seville, Spain, where she landed a full-time club gig as a folk singer. Dropping out of school, she continued performing in Europe and New York, eventually enlisting musician/producer Todd Rundgren to produce her debut album in 1990. After scoring a big hit with the self-revealing "I Kissed a Girl" from her 1995 self-titled album, she contributed new tracks to films and began performing on a variety of instruments, as on her 1997 release, *Happy Town*. Sobule most recently completed her new CD, *Pink Pearl*, on Beyond Records. Prior to releasing her record she toured with Lloyd Cole playing lead guitar.

The Music: Albums: *Things Here Are Different* (1990), *Jill Sobule* (1995), *Happy Town* (1997), *Pink Pearl* (2000)

Soundtrack Appearances: *The Truth About Cats and Dogs* (1996), *Harriet the Spy* (1996), *Mystery Men* (1999)

Did you know? Jill recorded songs for the films *Harriet the Spy* ("The Secretive Life"), *The Truth About Cats and Dogs* ("Where Do I Begin"), and *Grace of My Heart* ("Truth Is You Lied").

She received the Outstanding Song award (for "I Kissed a Girl") at the Gay and Lesbian Alliance Against Defamation (GLAAD) media awards.

> **JILL TALKS:**
> "Being of Jewish heritage, it's part of me. I recently asked a friend of mine, 'Would you have hidden me in your attic?' It's the ultimate expression of love you could ever offer someone."

Spector, center

Phil Spector

Born: December 26, 1940—New York, NY

Talent: Producer/label owner/songwriter/session musician

The Road to Fame: Phil entered the business in 1958 as the chief songwriter, lead guitarist, and background vocalist for the Teddy Bears, a one-hit wonder that recorded "To Know Him Is to Love Him." With the band's quick demise, he moved to New York and quickly became a successful songwriter/producer, turning out hit albums for the Ronettes, the Crystals, and several other all-girl groups. Phil's use of orchestral strings and horns in a rock context—better known as his "Wall of Sound" technique—became his widely copied signature. By the mid-1960s, he was producing bands like the Righteous Brothers and Ike and Tina Turner, but grew frustrated by declining record sales in the United States. After marrying Ronnie Bennett, the lead singer of the Ronettes, Phil took a lengthy hiatus in 1966, but he returned a few years later to work with the Beatles on *Let It Be* and on John Lennon's subsequent solo albums. Phil again retreated from the music industry in the late 1970s to live a quiet life.

The Music: **Phil as Producer:** "He's a Rebel" (1963, The Crystals), "Under the Moon of Love" (Curtis Lee), "Soul Man" (Calhoon), "The Long and Winding Road" (1970, The Beatles), "Instant Karma" (1975, John Lennon)

Phil as Songwriter: "There's No Other" (The Crystals), "Wait 'Til My Bobby Gets Home" (Darlene Love), "Be My Baby" (The Ronettes), "You've Lost That Lovin' Feelin'" (The Righteous Brothers), "River Deep—Mountain High" (Ike and Tina Turner), "Spanish Harlem" (Ben E. King)

Did you know? Phil slept in the office of mentors Jerry Leiber and Mike Stoller when he first arrived in New York.

Phil cowrote with legendary Brill Building writing teams Mann and Weil, Leiber and Stoller, and King and Goffin.

Phil befriended the Beatles and the Rolling Stones before the "British Invasion."

Paul Stanley

KISS

Born: Stanley Harvey Eisen, January
20, 1952—Queens, NY

Talent: Singer/songwriter/rhythm
guitarist

The Road to Fame: Only two years after receiving his first electric guitar, the fifteen-year-old Paul entered a New York recording studio to work on a project for Columbia Records. Though the album never came to fruition, Paul continued to study music in high school and joined a series of bands as lead vocalist and rhythm guitarist until meeting Gene Simmons in 1970. The two formed KISS in 1973, which would become the premier hard-rock band of the 1970s. In 1978, Paul and the three other members of KISS released solo albums on the same day in which they demonstrated their songwriting versatility. Paul is credited with keeping the band together during the 1980s, enabling it to survive in the 1990s and continue to thrive.

The Music: Hits: "Kissin' Time" (1974), "Hotter Than Hell" (1974), "Getaway" (1975), "Hard Luck Women" (1976), "God of Thunder" (1970), "Radioactive" (1978), "Lick It Up" (1987)

Influences: Elvis, Chuck Berry, the Rolling Stones, the Who, the Yardbirds

Did you know? Paul supported himself as a cab driver and kosher deli worker during his cover-band years.

The "Starchild"—Paul's stage character during KISS's makeup years—was derived from a character in Arthur C. Clarke's novel *2001: A Space Odyssey*.

In 1999, he was cast in the lead role in the Toronto production of Andrew Lloyd Webber's hit musical, *The Phantom of the Opera*.

Stein, second from right

Chris Stein

Blondie

Born: January 5, 1950 — Brooklyn, NY

Talent: Guitarist/songwriter/producer

The Road to Fame: Stein and girlfriend Deborah Harry formed Blondie in 1974, after departing the NYC neo-girl group the Stillettos. For Blondie, Stein wanted to mix the lush melodies of the classic 1960s girl-group sound with the fury and rawness inherent in the new punk rock. The group released two albums for the indie label Private Stock in the mid-1970s that were virtually ignored, save for the most devout skinny tie-wearing new wave fan. Fame did beckon after the band signed with the Chrysalis label, which released their 1978 breakthrough album, *Parallel Lines*. The band became international superstars thanks to their 1979 disco hit "Heart of Glass," and was able to maintain the pace over the course of several Top 10 hits and two more albums. The band's final album, 1982's *The Hunter*, marked the end of the band's chart-topping career, and Blondie broke up. In 1998, Stein and Harry reconvened the band for a new album, *No Exit*, and a subsequent tour.

The Music: Suggested Listening: *Parallel Lines* (1978), *Eat to the Beat* (1979), *Autoamerican* (1980)

Did you know? In 1983, Stein was diagnosed with pemphigus, a rare skin disorder that almost killed him. He recovered two years later.

Although he and Harry had ended their romantic relationship shortly after his recovery, the two continued to work together. Stein produced several of Harry's solo albums, including *Def, Dumb and Blonde*; *Debravation*; and *Rockbird*.

Stevens, left

Steve Stevens

Talent: Guitarist/composer

The Road to Fame: Guitar wunderkind Steve joined up with fledgling rocker Billy Idol in 1981 and went on to record three commercially successful albums with the singer until they parted ways in 1987. In addition to recording with some of the industry's top artists, Steve went on to contribute his wild guitar and compositional expertise to film soundtracks and solo projects. Recently, he has become something of a flamenco guitar aficionado.

The Music: Albums with Idol: *Billy Idol* (1982), *Rebel Yell* (1983), *Whiplash Smile* (1986)

Also Collaborated with: Ric Ocasek, the Thompson Twins, Joni Mitchell, Michael Jackson (on *Bad*), Harold Faltermeyer, Robert Palmer, Vince Neil

Solo and Group Efforts: *Steve Stevens' Atomic Playboys* (1989), *Black Light Syndrome* (with Tony Levin and Terry Bozzio, 1997)

On Film Soundtracks: *Top Gun* (1986), *Ace Ventura: Pet Detective* (1994), *Speed* (1994), *Assassins* (1996)

Did you know? Steve and Harold Faltermeyer won a 1986 Grammy for Best Instrumental Performance for the "Top Gun Anthem."

loomfield MarcBolan MICHAELBoltonIgorCavaleraLEONARD CO
an dannyelfman DONALDFAGEN PerryFarrellNickFeldman DougFei
ArtGarfunkel AdamGaynor GerryGoffin NINAGORDO
n SusannaHoffs ScottIan BillyJOEL MickJONES Ira Kapla
nnyKRAVITZ GettyLee JerryLeiber & Mike Stoller KEITHLev
rry Manilow DickManitoba BarryMANN Cynthia W
idler KeithMORRIS Randy Newman NOFX LauraNYRO LILO
thanRichman DavidLeeRoth ADAMSANDLER NeilSEDAKAJosh Sil
JillSobule PhilSpector PaulStanley ChrisSTEIN SteveST

Peter Stuart
Dog's Eye View

Talent: Singer/songwriter/guitarist

The Road to Fame: Beginning as an acoustic solo act, Peter worked his way through clubs and coffeehouses, eventually landing a backing vocalist slot with the Counting Crows on their 1994 tour. After opening for Tori Amos and Cracker, he formed the band Dog's Eye View, who subsequently landed a recording deal with Sony. "Everything Falls Apart," a single from their 1995 debut, *Happy Nowhere*, hit big the following year and brought the band to the mainstream.

The Music: Dog's Albums: *Happy Nowhere* (1995), *Small Wonders* (1996), *Daisy* (1997)

Did you know? Counting Crows frontman Adam Duritz—a good friend of Peter's—contributed background vocals to *Daisy*.

Max Weinberg

Born: April 13, 1951

Talent: Drummer/bandleader

The Road to Fame: Max's successful drumming career began when he joined Bruce Springsteen's E Street Band in the late 1970s, where he remained until 1988. Though he recorded eight albums and toured constantly with Bruce, Max still found time for session work with other musicians such as Meat Loaf, Barbra Streisand, Carole King, and Air Supply. In 1993, he became the leader of the Max Weinberg Seven, the house band for the show *Late Night with Conan O'Brien*, playing not only an active role in music direction but in the show's comedy bits as well.

The Music: **Big Albums with the Boss:** *Born to Run* (1975), *Darkness on the Edge of Town* (1978), *The River* (1980), *Born in the USA* (1984), *Tunnel of Love* (1987)

With Meat Loaf: *Bat Out of Hell* (1978), *Dead Ringer* (1981), *Midnight at the Lost & Found* (1983)

Did you know? Max performed for (and with) President Clinton at the 1993 and 1997 inaugural galas.

He rejoined Bruce Springsteen and the E Street Band at the Rock and Roll Hall of Fame dedication in 1995.

Max took his one-man drumming show, "An Evening with Max Weinberg," to over 150 colleges nationwide.

In 1990, he established Hard Ticket Entertainment, his own contemporary record label.

In 1999, Max returned to the E Street Band for Springsteen's year-long tour.

Weiss, right

Andrew Weiss
Rollins Band

Talent: Bassist/composer/producer

The Road to Fame: In 1987, Andrew left Gone—the instrumental outfit formed by former Black Flag guitarist Greg Ginn—in order to join Flag singer Henry Rollins's next project, the Rollins Band. He recorded four albums with the group, as well as a go-go-flavored side project with Rollins under the name Wartime (1990's *Fast Food for Thought*). He performed with the Rollins Band at the first Lollapalooza tour in 1991 before quitting two years later to take on production and session work with a number of groups.

The Music: Albums with the Rollins Band: *Life Time* (1988), *Do It* (1989), *Turned On* (1990), *The End of Silence* (1992)

Did you know? Andrew produced, mixed, and engineered four albums for the indie-alternative pranksters Ween.

He has performed and composed for artists as diverse as the Butthole Surfers, Psychic TV, the industrial-rock collective Pigface, and Yoko Ono.

In addition to bass, Andrew also plays keyboards and drums.

bAlpertJudahBauerBeastieBoys Beck RayBenson ERICBLOOM
mmyDavisJr. NEIL DIAMOND AdamDurwitz Bob Dylan Jak
sohFinn AlanFreed MartyFriedman JUSTINEFRISCHMANN Ken
terGreen BrettGurewitz RICHARDHELL GregHetson Peter Him
veKatz LenNYKaye CaroleKing MarkKnopfler ALKoop
Loeb CourtneyLove GARY LUCAS Mamasand the Papa
nfredMann Malcolm McClaren MC SEARCH NateMendel Ber
phenPerkins MoniquePowell Phranc JoeyRamone LouReed
e Simmons CARLYSIMON PaulSimon Slash Hillel SlovakDees

Brad Wilk

Rage Against the Machine

Born: September 5, 1968—Portland, OR

Talent: Drummer

The Road to Fame: Wilk—who once played with Eddie Vedder in his pre–Pearl Jam days—joined up with singer Zack de la Rocha, guitarist Tom Morello, and bassist Timmy C in 1992 to form Rage Against the Machine, the rock-rap-funk-metal powerhouse. The success of their self-titled 1993 debut motivated the band to highlight their somewhat radical left-wing image on their follow-up album, *Evil Empire* (1996). What little controversy that arose from their capitalism-bashing lyrics on the album was eclipsed by the disc's enormous sales. *The Battle of Los Angeles*, released in 1999, only cemented the band's reputation.

The Music: All the Rage: "Killing in the Name," "Bullet in the Head," "Bombtrack"

Did you know? Of the four members of Rage Against the Machine, it's been reported that Brad is the least political.

In interviews, Brad has talked of a connection to the number "3" throughout his life. He has a 3 tattooed on his left shoulder going down to his elbow.

Calling themselves "Shanti's Addiction," Brad and Tom Morello played "Calling Dr. Love" on the KISS tribute album *Kiss My Ass* with Maynard James Keenan of Tool and Billy Gould of Faith No More.

During a Lollapalooza show in Philadelphia, PA, in 1993, the four members of Rage walked out on stage naked with PMRC painted across their chests (one letter per person), electrical tape on their mouths, and with the guitars feeding back for fourteen minutes in protest of the Parents Musical Resource Council. The PMRC, as they were known, were a Washington, D.C., political group founded by Tipper Gore, Vice President Al Gore's wife, that promoted music censorship through stickers and ratings on albums. You can still find pictures taken during this protest on the Internet.

Carnie Wilson, left
Wendy Wilson, right

Carnie Wilson and Wendy Wilson

Wilson Phillips

Born: Carnie Wilson: April 29, 1968—Los Angeles, CA
Wendy Wilson: October 16, 1969—Los Angeles, CA

Talent: Singers/songwriters

The Road to Fame: The pop-rock vocal trio Wilson Phillips was the by-product of a failed charity project conceived in 1986 by Owen Elliot, daughter of Mama Cass Elliot. Sisters Carnie and Wendy and their friend Chynna Phillips secured a record deal in 1989, releasing their multi-platinum eponymous debut the following year. A 1992 follow-up release preceded their breakup, after which Chynna pursued a solo career and Carnie hosted a short-lived TV talk show. Both Wilson sisters continued to record together and collaborate with assorted artists.

The Music: Albums: *Wilson Phillips* (1990), *Shadows and Light* (1992)

Hit Singles: "Hold On," "You're in Love," "The Dream Is Still Alive," "Give It Up"

Did you know? Carnie and Wendy Wilson are the daughters of Brian Wilson of the Beach Boys.

The Wilson sisters taught Chynna Phillips how to harmonize just before forming Wilson Phillips.

The Wilson sisters have recorded background vocals with Belinda Carlisle, Billy Idol, Robert Palmer, and Brian Wilson.

The Wilson sisters are Jewish on their father's side.

Justman, top left
Wolf, top right

Peter Wolf and Seth Justman

The J. Geils Band

Born: Peter Blankfield: March 7, 1946—the Bronx, NY
Seth Justman: January 27, 1951—Washington, D.C.

Talent: Peter: Singer/songwriter
Seth: Keyboardist/singer/songwriter/producer

The Road to Fame: While working in Boston in 1967 as a DJ, Peter met guitarist Jerome Geils and joined Geils's new R&B–based rock band as their lead vocalist. Seth was recruited as the group's organist and primary songwriter in 1968, and over time, the J. Geils Band gained a loyal regional following and a record contract. Throughout the 1970s they reigned as one of the nation's premier touring bands, though they rarely scored radio hits. By 1982, having reached the pinnacle of their popularity with the previous year's *Freeze Frame* and its smash hit "Centerfold," tensions were mounting between Peter and Seth. With Peter's departure in 1983, Seth assumed the band's lead vocal duties, but a declining fan base ultimately led to the breakup of the band in 1985. Peter became a successful solo artist while Seth contributed his talents to other artists and continued to produce, as he had done for his former band.

The Music: Hit Albums: *The Morning After* (1971), *Bloodshot* (1973), *Nightmares . . . and Other Tales from the Vinyl Jungle* (1974), *Sanctuary* (1978), *Love Stinks* (1980), *Freeze Frame* (1981)

Hit Singles: "Centerfold," "Freeze Frame," "Looking for a Love," "Love Stinks," "Give It to Me," "Musta Got Lost"

Peter Goes Solo: *Lights Out* (1984), *Come As You Are* (1987), *Up to No Good* (1990), *Long Line* (1996)

Did you know? Seth was still an undergraduate student at Boston University when he joined the J. Geils Band.

Before becoming a singer, Peter was an acclaimed art student and painter who attended the prestigious University of Chicago and the Boston Museum School of Fine Arts.

Peter recorded duets with Mick Jagger and Aretha Franklin in the late 1980s.

Peter was briefly married to actress Faye Dunaway

Zal Yanovsky

The Lovin' Spoonful

Born: Zalman Yanovsky, January 19, 1944—Toronto, Ontario, Canada

Talent: Guitarist/singer/songwriter

The Road to Fame: Following a one-year stint in John Phillips' band the Mugwumps, Yanovsky formed the folk-rock band the Lovin' Spoonful with John Sebastian, Steve Boone, and Joe Butler in 1965. Though he left the band after a controversial drug arrest just two years later, Zal had recorded ten hit singles with the band. His post-Spoonful days included several solo projects and second guitar duties while touring with Kris Kristofferson and Sebastian during the 1970s.

The Music: Lovin' Albums: *Do You Believe in Magic* (1965), *Daydream* (1966), *Hums of the Lovin Spoonful* (1967)

A Spoonful of Hits: "Do You Believe in Magic," "Daydream," "Did You Ever Have to Make Up Your Mind," "Summer in the City," "You Didn't Have to Be so Nice"

Solo Hit: "As Long as You're Here"

Did you know? Yanofsky wrote the scores for two movies, Woody Allen's *What's Up Tiger Lily* (1966), and Francis Ford Coppola's *You're a Big Boy Now* (1967).

Yarrow, left

Peter Yarrow

Peter, Paul & Mary

Born: May 31, 1938 — New York, NY

Talent: Singer/songwriter/guitarist

The Road to Fame: In 1961, Peter formed a trio of folk vocalists with former Broadway singer Mary Travers and singer/comedian Noel "Paul" Stookey. The following year they were signed to Warner Brothers as Peter, Paul & Mary, releasing a self-titled debut that featured both original tunes ("Lemon Tree") and covers like the Weavers' hit "If I Had a Hammer." The following year they continued to rack up hits with "Puff the Magic Dragon" as well as Bob Dylan's "Blowin' in the Wind," which helped draw attention to the then little-known folk soloist. They enjoyed their lucrative collaboration until 1970, when they broke up to pursue individual solo careers. In 1978, they reunited briefly to record and tour. This on-again, off-again arrangement continued through the 1980s and 1990s and included various TV specials.

The Music: **Other Big Hits with P.P.M.:** "Stewball" (1963), "Tell It on the Mountain" (1963), "For Lovin' Me" (1965, recorded by Gordon Lightfoot), "Too Much of Nothing" (1968, Bob Dylan), "Leaving on a Jet Plane" (1967, Bob Denver)

Awards: 1962 Grammys for Best Performance by a Vocal Group and Best Folk Recording for their debut; 1969 Grammy for their children's record *Peter, Paul and Mommy*

Did you know? Peter, Paul & Mary witnessed Martin Luther King's "I Have a Dream" speech with Dylan at the march in Washington, D.C., in March 1963.

Until the Beatles arrived, Peter's trio was the most popular vocal ensemble in the United States.

Warren Zevon

Born: January 24, 1947—Chicago, IL

Talent: Singer/songwriter/pianist/guitarist

The Road to Fame: Warren studied classical piano as a child, but his tumultuous family life soon drove him to rock and roll. By the late 1960s, he was in Los Angeles doing session work and recording his unsuccessful self-titled 1969 solo debut. In 1976, after writing commercial jingles and a stint as the Everly Brothers' pianist, Warren's friend Jackson Browne secured him a deal with Asylum Records. His second album with the label, *Excitable Boy*, showcased his cynical wit and dark satire and won both cult and commercial victories. Though Warren fell prey to alcoholism, he survived the early 1980s and reemerged from the shadows in 1986 with members of R.E.M. for a studio project dubbed the Hindu Love Gods. The appearance of his hit "Werewolves in London" in the film *The Color of Money* also helped to solidify his comeback, allowing him to continue recording such cult favorites as *Mr. Bad Example* and *Mutineer* throughout the 1990s.

The Music: Breakthrough Single: "Werewolves in London" (1978); it was Warren's only hit single.

Essential Recordings: *Excitable Boy* (1978), *Sentimental Hygiene* (1987), *Dr. Bad Example* (1991)

Did you know? As a child, Warren studied piano with composer Igor Stravinsky.

At age sixteen, he stole his father's Corvette and drove to New York to become a folk singer.

Linda Ronstadt covered three of Warren's songs on her 1974 album *Hasten Down the Wind*, which was named after one of these singles.

Neil Young, Bob Dylan, members of R.E.M., and George Clinton appeared on *Sentimental Hygiene*.

Warren wrote the sarcastic "Even a Dog Can Shake Hands," the theme to *Action*, the short-lived television show that satirized the movie industry.

> **WARREN ON MUSIC:**
> "Going to a 7-Eleven in the middle of the night and hearing the clerk whistling one of my songs—that's my idea of a great cover version."

John Zorn

Born: September 2, 1953—New York, NY

Talent: Composer/arranger/alto saxophonist/pianist

The Road to Fame: Referred to by ardent fans and hissing critics as "the anti–Kenny G," Zorn's musical aesthetics are informed by everything from classic jazz progenitors (such as John Coltrane, Albert Ayler, Ornette Coleman) and cartoon scores (Carl Stalling, Raymond Scott) to traditional klezmer music and extreme underground rock. Early in his career, he pioneered the creation of improvisational "game pieces" in which the conductor directs the players through a series of rules similar to those found in regulation sports. In the early 1990s, Zorn embraced hardcore punk culture with his repertory bands Naked City and Spy Vs. Spy (the former group mixed as many as forty-four different types of genres in a song less than a minute long, while the latter delivered versions of Ornette Coleman songs in blistering thrash tempos), and he has applied free jazz aesthetics to ambient music in Painkiller, his group with Bill Laswell and Mick Harris. In 1994, he formed the quartet Masada, an amalgam of klezmer, avant-garde, and traditional jazz music that has released over ten records to international acclaim as a benchmark of American jazz. There are very few musical genres to which Zorn hasn't applied his vision, and by breaking down the walls of so-called "exclusive" music styles, he has cemented his reputation as a true renaissance performer.

The Music: **Essential Recordings:** *The Big Gundown* (1984, reissued in 2000), *Spillane* (1986), *Spy Vs. Spy: The Music of Ornette Coleman* (1988), *Naked City* (1989), *Masada, Vol. 2: Beit* (1995)

Did you know? Zorn runs two record labels, Avant (based in Japan) and Tzadik (based in New York City). He is fluent in Japanese and lives in Japan six months out of the year.

Tzadik's Radical New Jewish Culture series features works by traditional klezmer and avant-garde Jewish musicians in an effort to promote awareness and create a dialogue addressing modern Jewish culture.

The advertising agency Weiden & Kennedy frequently asks Zorn to compose music for commercials. The deal is structured so that the composer gets paid whether the music is used or not.

Even when performing in energetic and sometimes grueling playing situations, Zorn frequently wears his prayer clothes under his T-shirt and camouflage fatigues onstage.

Afterword

by Peretz (Perry) Farrell

Last night I sat with a friend has a tremendous passion for searching out the truth. He is a very intense fellow who sometimes leans a bit far out with his conspiracy theories. We discussed different topics, varying from the origins of HIV virus to real cures for cancer. He believes that a lot of misinformation is being disseminated by pharmaceutical corporations who want to drive the drug industry. As the night grew more and more heated my friend began bearing down on a theory that Jesus never existed, nor did Moses. He claimed that they were invented by the powers that be to control the masses. That people need myths. Something to believe in. The Bible, he said, was written and edited by so many people that there isn't any real truth to it.

Here was a fellow that I enjoyed speaking with, and I appreciated his thirst for knowledge. But at that moment I broke down. I said to him "You know when you tell me that the Bible was invented by someone . . . and it never happened, that is like telling me that I am not real, because you are speaking about my family. Because that book is a history of my family. My name, Peretz, was chosen in honor of one of those relatives. You see, the Jewish people, whether they understand it or not, are living proof that they are not myths but real history. And because we are kept alive this very day is in fact proof that God exists because, if it weren't for his intervention, we wouldn't be here. And that is a reason to praise his name."

I study the Torah. And when a person tells me that the Torah is a book written by some man, I tell him, "When explored, the Torah is an operating system that has overtures to genetics, music, and metaphysics."

To understand what you really have in your hands when you hold the Torah inspires awe. The author is divine.

Leviticus 25: "Sound the trumpet throughout your land. Consecrate the fiftieth year and proclaim liberty throughout the land for all its inhabitants; it shall be a jubilee for you."

The pasha Behar in Vayikra (Leviticus 25–27) has inspired me above all other writings, and I am working to bring in the Jubilee for our generation.

King David was a famous musician before becoming king. He would go out to the people and sing. He had a harp that he kept by his bed and it would begin to resonate at night. In the years before he became king, he wrote and sang the ultimate blues. He had more people chasing him than the hairs on his head and thus began the writing of the Psalms, songs written in longing for a kingdom.

There are nine songs that are called holy
The first, was written by Adam
After he was cast down to earth
God forgave him and the Sabbath came
He was so overjoyed
He wrote "A song of the Sabbath day"
The children of Israel began singing when
The sea was split before them and they were
freed from Egypt . . .
The last of the holy songs written
was by King Solomon
called "Holy of Holies" because it
spoke of love and consummation.
Inspired by the completion of the Temple
Scholars debate whether God loved the Temple
or the Song more . . .
In our most ecstatic moments
man raises up to song.
There is a song ahead
that has not yet been sung.
This song, they say
will be sung by the children of exile
and that the mountains
and trees,
every blade of grass will resonate
in harmony
and that song will come at last
with redemption.

Photo credits

Page 53: Michael Ochs Archives/Venice, CA

Page 54: Chris Walter/Retna Pictures, Ltd.

Page 55: Michael Ochs Archives/Venice, CA

Page 56: Gary Gershoff/Retna Pictures, Ltd.

Page 57: Gavin Smith/Retna Pictures, Ltd.

Page 58: Laura Brunelliere

Page 59: Gary Gershoff/Retna Pictures, Ltd.

Page 60: Chuck Krall/Michael Ochs
Archives/Venice, CA

Page 61: Govert De Roos/Sunshine/Retna
Pictures, Ltd.

Page 62: Michael Ochs Archives/Venice, CA

Page 63: Gavin Evans/Retna Pictures, Ltd.

Page 64: Gary Spector/Columbia Records/
Adler Archives

Page 65: Martyn Goodacre/Retna Pictures, Ltd.

Page 66: Warner Brothers Records

Page 67: Chris Toliver/Retna Pictures, Ltd.

Page 68: Michael Ochs Archives/Venice, CA

Page 69: Michael Ochs Archives/Venice, CA

Page 70: Michael Ochs Archives/Venice, CA

Page 71: Jay Blakesberg/Retna Pictures, Ltd.

Page 72: Michael Ochs Archives/Venice, CA

Page 73: Tim Hale/Retna Pictures, Ltd.

Page 74: Michael Ochs Archives/Venice, CA

Page 75: Kees Tabak/Retna Pictures, Ltd.

Page 76: Michael Ochs Archives/Venice, CA

Page 77: Michael Putland/Retna Pictures, Ltd.

Page 78: Chris Walker/Retna Pictures, Ltd.

Page 79: Steve Eichner/Retna Pictures, Ltd.

Page 80: Michael Ochs Archives/Venice, CA

Page 81: Vincent Soyez/Used by permission of
Roadrunner Records

Page 82: Fin Costello/Redferns/Retna
Pictures, Ltd.

Page 84: Michael Ochs Archives/Venice, CA

Page 85: BMI Photo Archives/Michael Ochs
Archives/Venice, CA

Page 86: Steve Granitz/Retna Pictures, Ltd.

Page 87: James Slovak/Slim Skinny Productions

Page 88: Chris Walter/Retna Pictures, Ltd.

Page 89: Debra Rothenberg /Retna
Pictures, Ltd.

Page 90: Ray Avery/Shooting Star

Page 91: Fin Costello/Retna Pictures, Ltd.

Page 92: Michael Ochs Archives/Venice, CA

Page 93: James Shive/Retna Pictures, Ltd.

Page 94: Youri Lenquette/Retna Pictures, Ltd.

Page 95: Scott Weiner/Retna Pictures, Ltd.

Page 96: Naomi Peterson/Courtesy of SST
Records

Page 97: Wilfred/A.P.R.F./Shooting Star

Page 98: Carraro/Stills/Retna Pictures, Ltd.

Page 99: Michael Ochs Archives/Venice, CA

Page 100: Michael Ochs Archives/Venice, CA

Page 101: Michael Ochs Archives/Venice, CA

Page 102: John Atashian/Retna Pictures, Ltd.

Page 103: Michael Delsol

oomfield Marc Bolan MICHAEL Bolton Igor Cavalera LEONARD COF
an danny elfman DONALD FAGEN Perry Farrell Nick Feldman Doug Feig
rt Garfunkel Adam Gaynor Gerry Goffin NINA GORDO
n Susanna Hoffs Scott Ian Billy JOEL Mick JONES Ira Kapla
my KRAVITZ Getty Lee Jerry Leiber & Mike Stoller KEITH Lev
rry Manilow Dick Manitoba Barry MANN Cynthia WI
dler Keith MORRIS Randy Newman NOFX Laura NYRO PHIL Oc
han Richman David Lee Roth ADAM SANDLER Neil SEDAKA Josh Silv
Jill Sobule Phil Spector Paul Stanley Chris STEIN STEVE STEV
DY WILSON Peter WOLF Peter Ya